RECAPTURE OF GUAM

1944 BATTLE AND LIBERATION OF GUAM

DANIEL WRINN

CONTENTS

GET YOUR FREE COPY OF WW2: SPIES, SNIPERS AND THE WORLD AT WAR

Never miss a new release by signing up for my free readers group. Learn of special offers and interesting details I find in my research. You'll also get WW2: Spies, Snipers and Tales of the World at War delivered to your inbox. (You can unsubscribe at any time.) Go to danielwrinn.com to sign up.

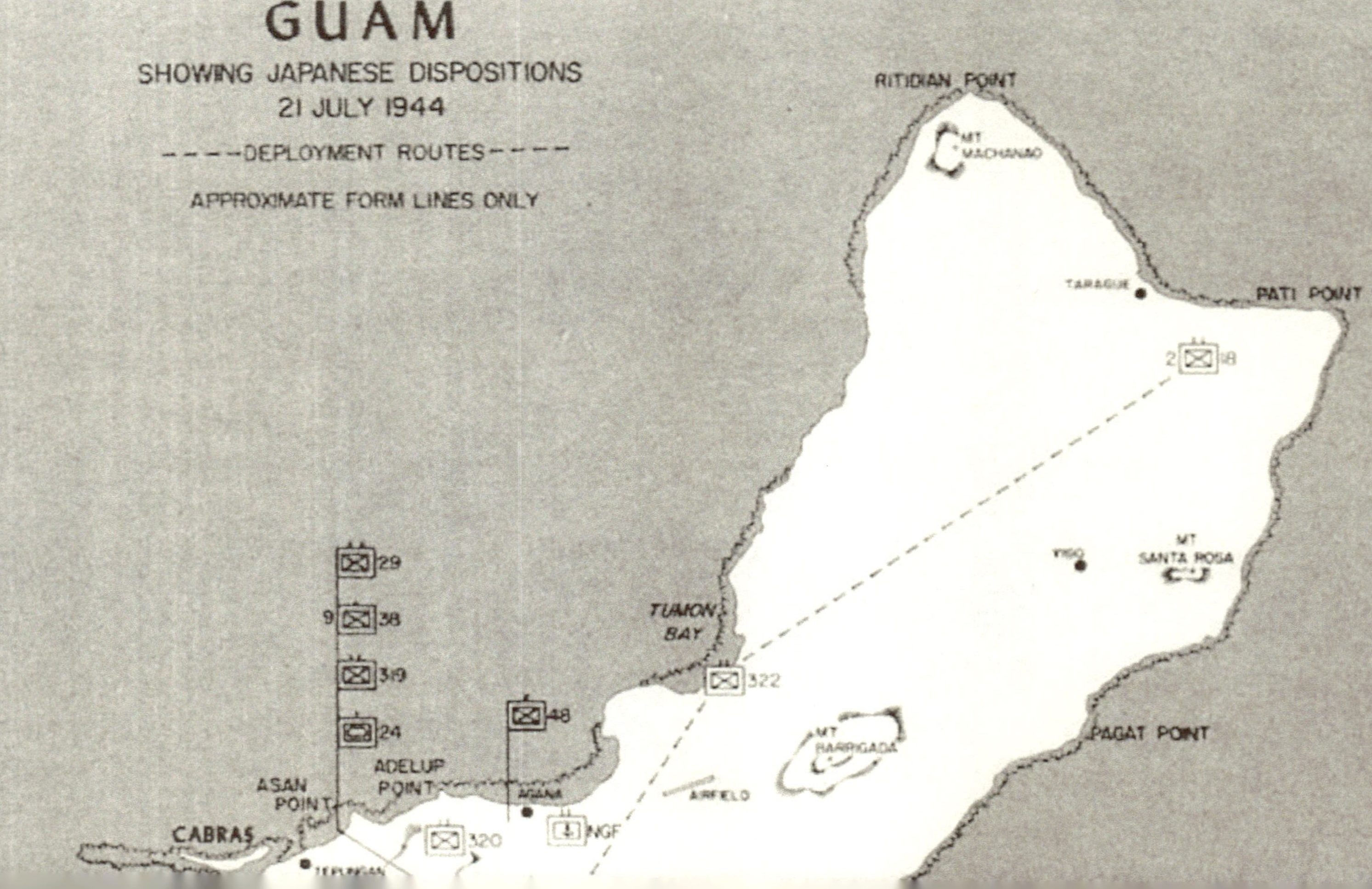

GUAM
SHOWING JAPANESE DISPOSITIONS
21 JULY 1944
DEPLOYMENT ROUTES
APPROXIMATE FORM LINES ONLY
RITIDIAN POINT
MT MACHANAO
TARAGUE
PATI POINT
2 18
YIGO
MT SANTA ROSA
TUMON BAY
322
MT BARRIGADA
PAGAT POINT
AIRFIELD
29
9 38
319
48
24
ADELUP POINT
ASAN POINT
AGANA
NGF
CABRAS
320
TEPUNGAN

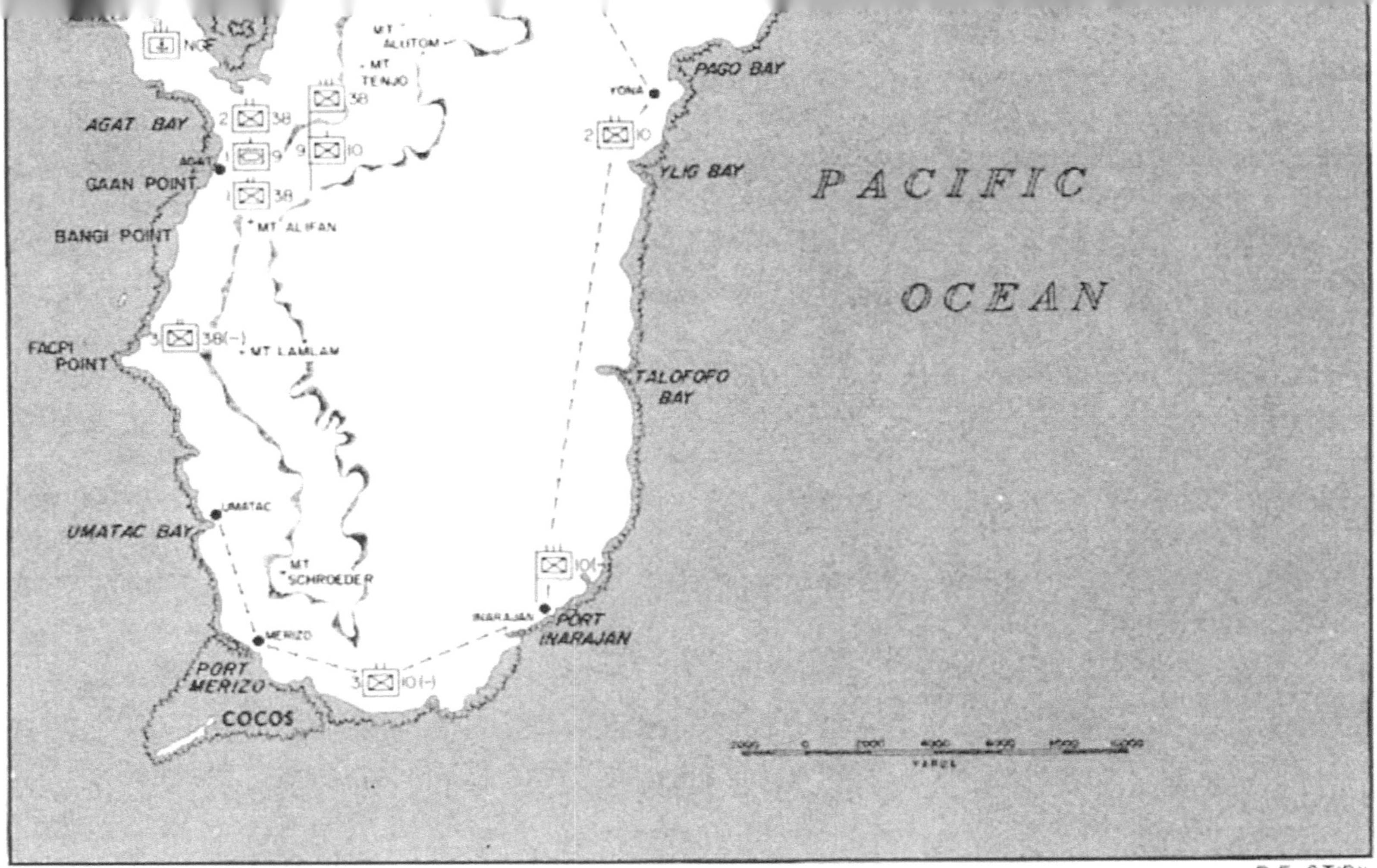

PACIFIC
OCEAN
PAGO BAY
YLIG BAY
TALOFOFO BAY
YONA
AGAT BAY
GAAN POINT
AGAT
BANGI POINT
FACPI POINT
UMATAC BAY
UMATAC
PORT MERIZO
MERIZO
COCOS
PORT INARAJAN
INARAJAN
MT ALUTOM
MT TENJO
MT ALIFAN
MT LAMLAM
MT SCHROEDER
NGF
CP3
2 38
38
1 9
9 10
1 38
3 38(-)
2 10
10(-)
3 10(-)
YARDS
R F STIBIL

BACK TO GUAM

After a two-hour bombardment from six battleships, nine cruisers, and a handful of destroyers hammering the wrinkled black hills, cliffs, rice patties, and caves facing the attacking fleet on the west side of the island—liberation day began at 0530 on July 21, 1944.

Flames fountained from 14-inch guns belching thunder and fire. Setting off a spectacular blossom of flame on the inland hillsides and fields. The glow from the star shells illuminated the shore, the ships, and the troops lining the rails of the LSTs (Landing Ships, Tank), bringing the soldiers and Marines back to Guam.

The daylight shelling was enhanced by the bombing and strafing of carrier fighters, torpedo planes, and bombers for the pre-landing softening up. Task Force 58 had blasted Guam's airfield since June 11, while other bombardments had started as early as May 6.

Marine assault troops laden with fighting gear, and bayonets bulging from their packs, enjoyed their traditional Marine pre-landing breakfast of steak and eggs. The loudspeakers echoed: "Now hear this. . . Now hear this." Unit commanders on board the LSTs visited with their Marines and double-checked their gear. They straightened packs, gave encouraging pats on the shoulder, and squared away the lines of Marines going below to the well decks before boarding the LVTs (Landing Vehicles, Tracked).

Troops on board the attack transports went over the rail and down cargo nets. Weighed down with forty-plus pound packs and weapons—they held on for their lives. They clambered into their LCVPs (Landing Craft, Vehicle, Personnel) or Higgin's boats. If all went as planned, these troops would transfer from the landing craft to the LVTs at the reef's edge.

Aircraft roared overhead. Navy guns thundered a deafening background noise. The voice of Major General Roy Geiger, commander of III Amphibious Corps, boomed: "You've been honored. The nation watches you go to battle to liberate this former American bastion from the enemy. The honor bestowed on you is a signal one. May the glorious traditions of the Marine Corps esprit de corps spur you to victory. You have been honored."

On board the crowded and muggy well decks of the LSTs, troops climbed on board the LVTs. They waited in a hell of claustrophobia until the LSTs' bow doors dropped. The loaded LVTs rattled out over the ramps into the swell of the sea. Amphibian tractors circled near the lines of departure while a flight of attack craft from the *Wasp* drowned the amtrac engines' whine, whirling up clouds of fire and dust obscuring the landing beaches. Fifty-three torpedo planes, sixty-five bombers, and eighty-five fighters executed a bombing sweep and grass-cutting strafing along the northern landing beaches of Agana, heading south toward Bangi Point.

Task Force 53 commander, Admiral Richard Conolly, said: "I aim to get the troops ashore standing up." Conolly earned the nickname "Close-in Conolly" from his insistence on having naval gunfire support ships fire very close in to the beaches.

Private First Class James Helt was a radio man in the bow of an LVT moving toward shore. He later wrote about how he wondered if anything could still be alive on Guam.

Colonel Hideyuki Takeda, a staff officer in the defending *29th Division*, wrote the island could only be defended if the Americans did not land. In his diary, he also noted that the only respite from the barrage was a "stiff drink."

The bold and brave Navy UDT (Underwater Demolition Teams) cleared all the beach obstacles for the assault. Navy Chief James Chittum noted these pathfinders were often close enough to draw small arms fire. They exploded 650 wire obstacle cages filled with cemented coral on Asan. On Agat, they detonated a 200-foot hole for unloading in the coral reef. Navy UDT teams also removed half of a small freighter blocking the channel from the assault. Scouts and swimmers left a sign for this first assault wave at Asan: "Welcome Marines—USO This way."

At 0730, a flare was fired overhead the waiting flotilla. Admiral Conolly ordered: "Land the Landing Force." The first wave of the 3rd Marine Division broke the circle of waiting LVTs and formed a line to cross the 2,000 yards of water to the beach between Asan and Adelup. By 0830, the first elements of the 3rd Marine Division were on Guam. Less than five minutes later, the lead assault troops of the 1st Provisional Marine Brigade crossed the shell-cratered strand at Agat, six miles south of the beachhead at Asan-Adelup.

OPERATION FORAGER PLANNING

In late 1943, the Joint Chiefs of Staff decided to advance the direction of the Pacific War. In command of the Southwest Pacific, General MacArthur was ordered to head north through New Guinea to regain the Philippines. Admiral Nimitz, commander-in-chief of the US Pacific Fleet, proposed to move through the Central Pacific to secure a hold in the Marianas.

The strategic bombing of Japan would originate from captured airfields on Guam, Saipan, and Tinian. The new strategic weapon for the attacks would be the B-29 bomber with a range of 3,000 miles and the ability to carry over 10,000 pounds of bombs. The codename for this Marianas operation was "Forager." The drive in the Central Pacific started with the landings on Tarawa in November 1943. Followed by landings on Roi-Namur, Eniwetok, and Kwajalein.

Admiral Nimitz finalized his plans for Guam in 1944. He selected his command structure for the Marianas campaign. Admiral Spruance, coming off a tremendous victory at

Midway, was designated Commander of the Fifth Fleet and all the Central Pacific Task Forces. Spruance would command all units involved in Operation Forager.

Admiral Turner, who had commanded naval forces at Guadalcanal's landings, was to head Task Force 51. Admiral Turner would also command the northern attack force for the invasion of Saipan and Tinian. Admiral Connolly who'd commanded the invasion forces at Roi-Namur in the Marshalls, would lead the southern attack force—Task Force 53 assigned to Guam.

General Holland Smith, the expeditionary troop commander for the Marianas, would be responsible for the northern troops and landing forces on Saipan and Tinian. Marine General Roy Geiger, an aviator who had conducted the Bougainville operation, would command the southern troops and the III Amphibious Corps landing forces on Guam.

Guam's invasion was originally set for June 18, the 3rd Marine Division, the 1st Provisional Marine Brigade, and the Army's 77th Infantry Division would lead the assault, but the 3rd and 1st Marine Division were held in floating reserve until the course of operations on Saipan became clear. The 77th stood by on Oahu, ready to be called in if needed.

Admiral Spruance kept the floating reserves southeast of Saipan, out of the path of any Japanese naval attack. A powerful Japanese fleet was eager to clash with the American invasion force and descended on the Mariana Islands. The opposing carrier groups fought it out nearby in the battle of the Philippine Sea, one of the most critical battles of the Pacific War. The Japanese Imperial Navy lost over 300 planes out of the 430 launched in the fight. On June 19, the clash would be forever known as "the Great Marianas Turkey Shoot." It was a catastrophe for the Japanese and ended once and for all any enemy air or naval threat to the Mariana Islands invasion.

The brutal fighting on Saipan eventually shifted in favor of the American Marines and soldiers battling the Japanese. The US Navy was now ready to direct their attention to Guam, currently slated to receive the most thorough pre-landing bombardment yet seen in the Pacific War.

After weeks at sea, the 3rd Division and 1st Brigade were given a break and a chance to lose their sea legs. The Task Force 53 convoy moved back to Eniwetok atoll, where a twenty-mile-wide lagoon became the forward naval base.

Marines welcomed the break and walked on the island's dry land—there was even warm beer to all those onshore. The Marine veterans of New Georgia, Eniwetok, and Bougainville had a chance to look over the soldiers from the Army's 77th Infantry Division arriving from Oahu. The recapture of Guam named W-Day was now set for July 21.

The 3rd Marine Division, under General Allen H. Turnage, had received their baptism of fire on Bougainville in November 1943 and spent the remaining months on Guadalcanal training and absorbing casualty replacements. The 1st Provisional Marine Brigade, organized on Guadalcanal, was also a veteran outfit. One of its infantry regiments, the 4th Marines, was formed from a disbanded raider battalion who'd fought in the Solomons. The III Amphibious Corps was prepared to land over 53,000 Marines, soldiers, and sailors.

General Takashina, commanding the Japanese *29th Infantry Division,* waited for the attack and was sure it would come, but he didn't know from where. The *29th* served in Manchuria until it was sent to the Marianas in February 1944. Its *18th Regiment* fell victim to an American submarine, the *Trout,* and lost 2,237 of its 3,000 men when the transport was sunk. They reorganized on Saipan, and the *18th Infantry Regiment* took two infantry battalions to Guam together with two tank companies.

Another regiment from the *29th*, garrisoned on Tinian, the *38th Infantry*, arrived on Guam in March. Other major Japanese defending units were the *10th Independent Mixed Regiment* and the *48th Independent Mixed Brigade* formed on Guam in March. With supporting troops, the Japanese defending forces numbered 11,000 men. Add to these 5,000 naval troops of the *54th Keibitai Guard Force* and 2,000 naval airmen reorganized as infantry to defend the Orote peninsula.

General Takashina was in overall tactical command of the 18,000 Army and Navy defenders. His immediate superior was General Obata, commanding the *31st Army* also on Guam, but not intentionally. Obata was trapped on Guam by the American landing on Saipan after making an inspection trip to the Palau Islands. He left the defense of Guam to Takashina.

It was no secret to the Japanese that the Americans planned to assault Guam. The invasion of Saipan and month-long bombardment by ships and planes left only the questions of when and where. With fifteen miles of potential landing beaches along the west coast, the Japanese couldn't be very wrong no matter where they decided to defend.

Tokyo Rose said they expected the Americans. On board ship, American troops heard her pleasant, beguiling voice on the radio while she made threats of dire things waiting to happen to the invasion troops. But she was never taken seriously by any of her American "fans."

General Kiyoshi Shigematsu, attempting to bolster the morale of his *48th Independent Mixed Brigade*, told his men: "the enemy is overconfident because of his successful landing on Saipan. They are now planning a reckless attack on Guam. We have an excellent opportunity to annihilate them on the beaches."

Hideki Tojo, Prime Minister of Japan, also had feisty words for his commanders: "The fate of Japan depends on the result of your operation, inspire the spirit of your officers and men to the very end. Continue to destroy the enemy gallantly and persistently—alleviate the anxiety of the emperor."

Fifty years later, a former Japanese lieutenant wrote of the incredible American invasion fleet offshore had "paved the sea" and recalled what he thought on July 21: "this is the day I will die."

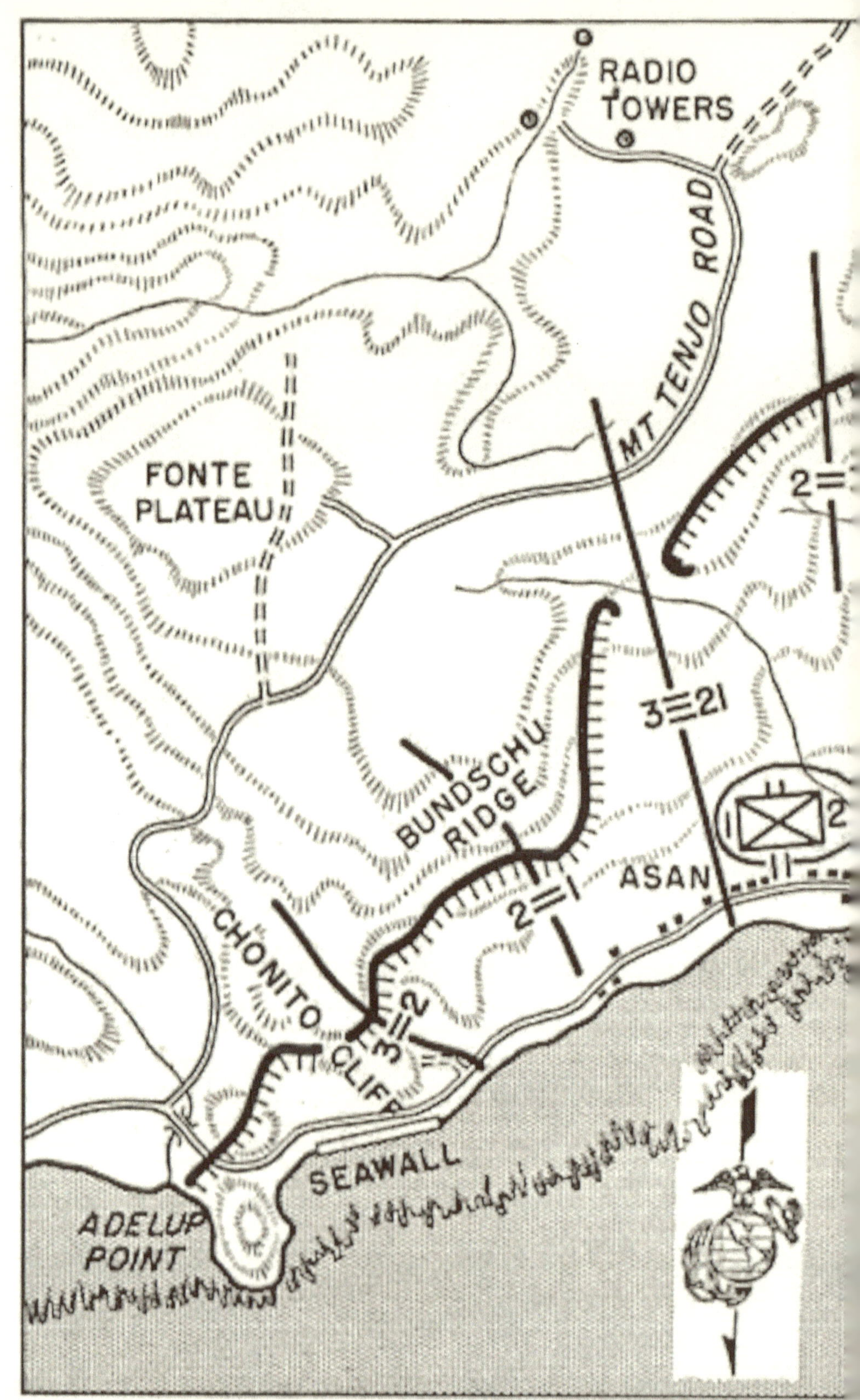

RADIO
TOWERS
MT TENJO ROAD
FONTE
PLATEAU
2
3≡21
BUNDSCHU
RIDGE
2
2≡1
ASAN
CHONITO CLIFF
3≡2
SEAWALL
ADELUP
POINT

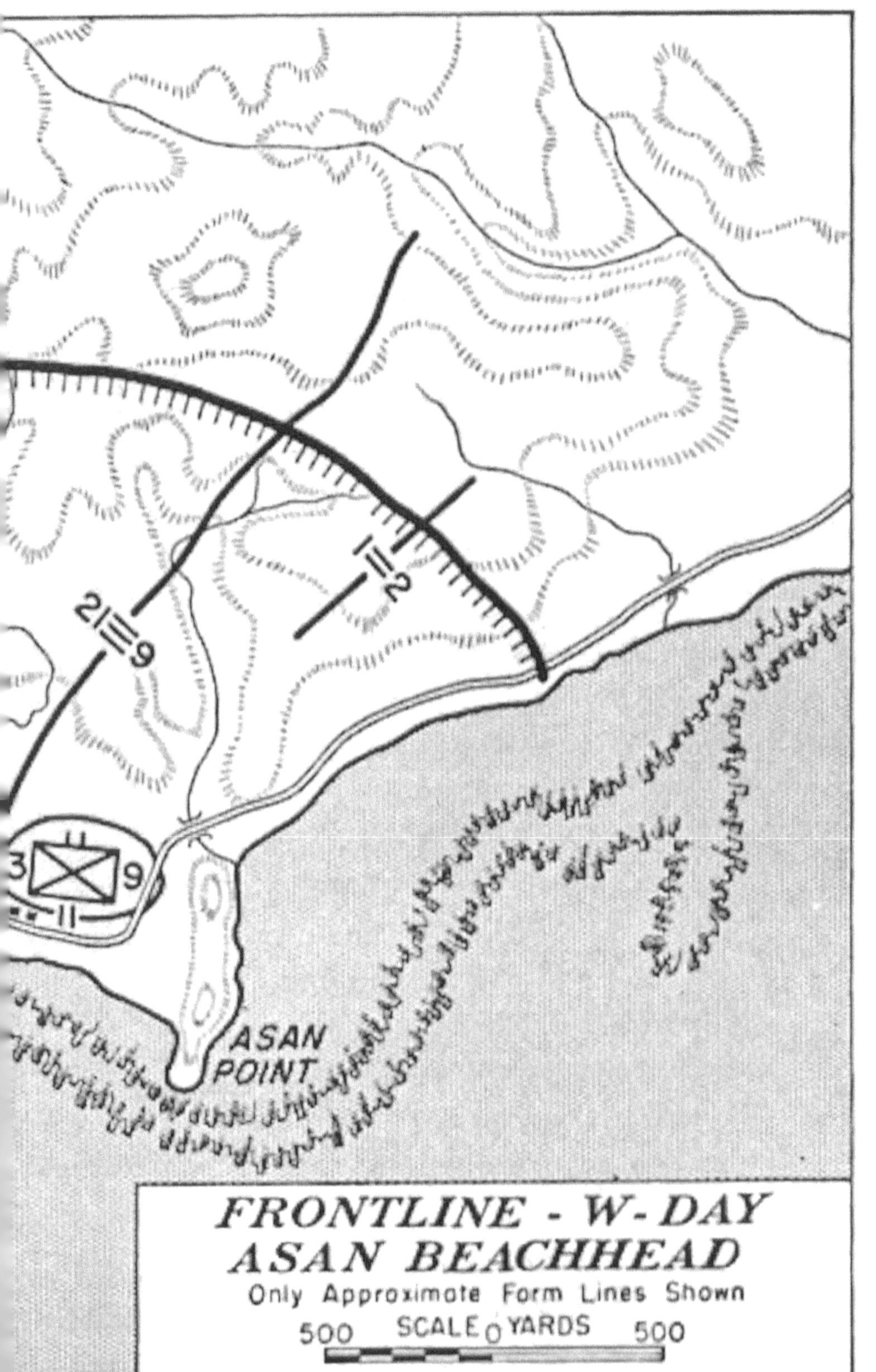

2≡9
2≡2
3 X 9
ASAN POINT
FRONTLINE - W- DAY
ASAN BEACHHEAD
Only Approximate Form Lines Shown
500   SCALE 0 YARDS   500

W-DAY IN THE NORTH

The 3rd Marine Division troops landed practically into the lap of General Takashina's U-shaped command post. The CP cave was carved out of sandstone cliff that overlooked the Asan-Adelup beachhead. Its looming heights dominated the beaches where the 3rd and 21st Marines were headed in for their assault.

W-Day on July 21, 1944, started as a beautiful day. But it soon turned hazy as the violent clouds of dust, smoke, and fire fountained into the sky. At 0805 an observer shouted into his microphone: "First wave on the beach." At 0833, the same man confirmed the battle was on and announced: "Troops ashore on all beaches."

The 3rd Marines struck out on the far left of the 2,500-yard beachhead toward Bundschu Ridge. Also known as Chonito Cliff, it had high, difficult ground that needed to be taken before the final beachhead line or the first goal of the landing could be achieved. The 21st Marines went straight up the middle. They advanced inland, securing the line of cliffs and defending them until the division caught up and could expand the beachhead outward. The 9th Marines landed on the right flank near Asan Point and moved inland over patties and across lower and easier to traverse hills, but all part of the same formidable enemy held ridgeline.

The 3/9 Marines took intense fire from the front and right flank near Asan Point and called in tanks for help. One company got to the ridge ahead of the others and threw the enemy off balance, making the regiments advance easier. The 9th Marines smashed through their initial objectives quickly and had to slacken their advance as to not thin out the division's lines.

The 21st Marines, in a stroke of luck later called unbelievable, found two unguarded defiles on both sides of the regiment's action zone. The 21st climbed straight to the clifftops and formed a bridge covering both defiles. This allowed the 2nd and 3rd Battalions to form a bridge covering both defiles while the 1st Battalion swept the area underneath the cliffs.

The 12th Marines were swiftly landed on the beach with

their burdensome guns and equipment. The 3rd Battalion was registered and firing by noon. By1620, every battery was in position and ready to support the offensive. According to Captain Austin Gattis of the 12th Marines: "We must attribute the success of our regiment setting up so quickly to training—because we'd done it over and over. It was an efficiency learned and practiced and it always gave the 12th a leg up."

On the left flank, the 3rd Marines got the worst of the enemy resistance. They took intense artillery and mortar fire coming in on the beaches, as well as advancing through the toughest terrain. Japanese machine gun fire laced with interlocking bands made the approaches to the steep cliffs deadly. The enemy defenders knew how to use their weapons well. Japanese troops would roll grenades down the escarpment onto the Marines. Snipers found protection and refuge in the countless folds and ridges of irregular terrain. The ridge tops were arrayed like breastworks of some nightmarish medieval castle. As if ten Japanese soldiers on top could hold off a hundred Marines below.

Japanese Lieutenant Kenichi Itoh wrote in his diary that even with a terrible bombardment he felt secure his countrymen could hold and possibly even win. He later wrote about that eventful day in July 1944, after the war. Lieutenant Itoh thought it was all a bad dream, and "absurd" to think that his forces could ever have withstood that onslaught.

On W-Day the 3/3 Marines were on the extreme left flank of the line facing Adelup Point. Marines seized territory in their zone with support from tanks and half-track-mounted 75mm guns. A little nose projecting from Chonito Ridge held up the regimental advance. Company A, under the command of Captain Geary Bundschu was able to secure a foothold within 100 yards of the promontory crest, but failed to hold their position in the face of intense machine gun fire. Captain

Bundschu called for corpsmen and stretchers. He also requested permission to disengage, but his request was refused, and he was ordered to hold what he had.

The attack was ordered to continue in the afternoon under cover of a massive 81mm mortar barrage. No 2nd Battalion companies could gain any ground beyond what they already held. The Japanese *320th Independent Infantry Battalion* fought fiercely and held fast.

Two hours later, Company A was ordered to make another attack, according to a Marine Combat correspondent: "When the attack at 1700 went off, there was no change. The Marines made little progress. Company A attacked again and again and again. They reached the top but failed to hold. After Captain Bundschu was killed, his company slid back to their former positions."

Throughout the days of brutal fighting, Marines attempted to envelop the Japanese in a pincer movement using companies A and C. On regimental orders, the assault started at 1100—but got nowhere at first. Company A got to the top but was thrown off. Company E advanced slowly. But after several probes into the Japanese resistance, Marines found the enemy was weakening.

By 1900, Company E Marines reached the top above Company A's position. The Japanese had finally pulled back. A further Marine advance confirmed the enemy's withdrawal.

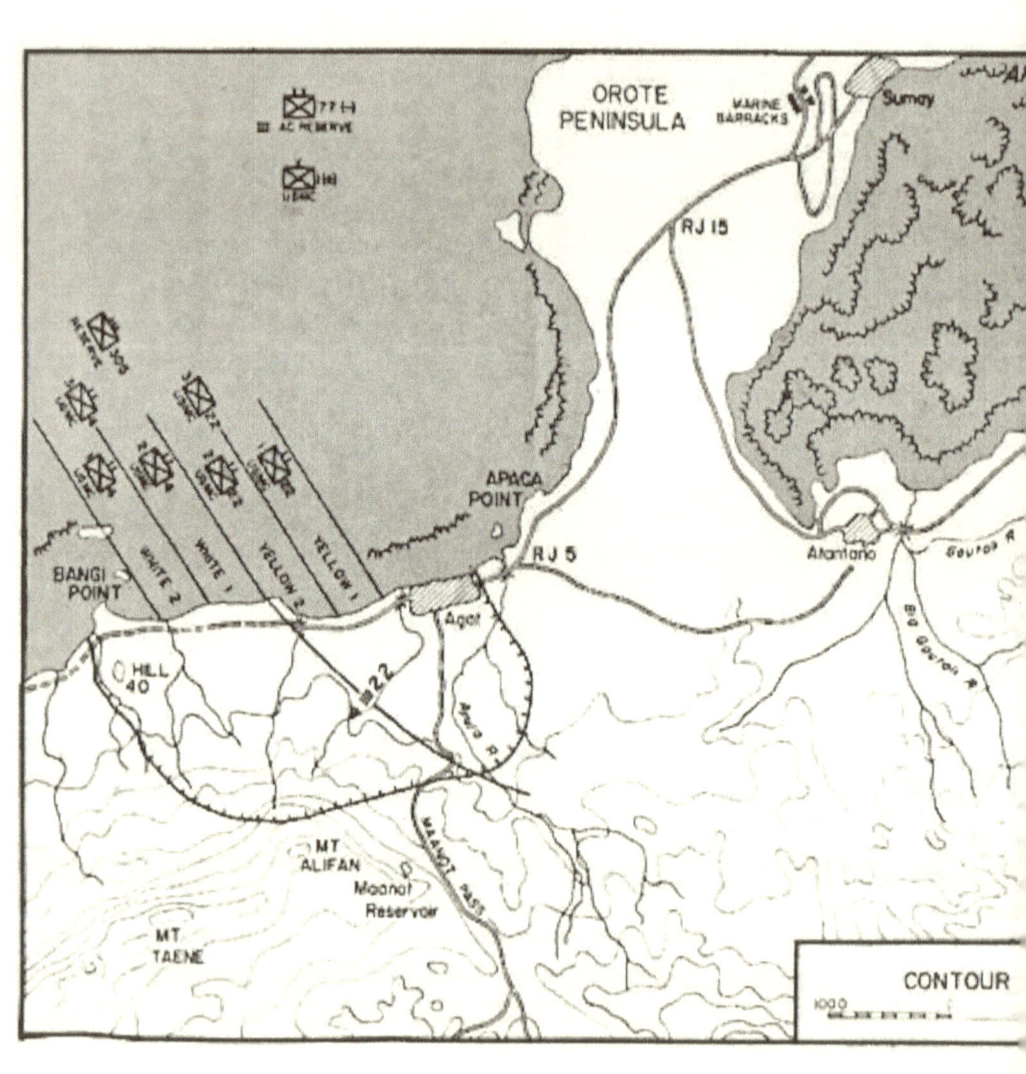
OROTE
PENINSULA
MARINE
BARRACKS
Sumay
RJ 15
77
III AC RESERVE
(Inf)
APACA
POINT
RJ 5
Atantano
Agat
BANGI
POINT
WHITE 2
WHITE 1
YELLOW 2
YELLOW 1
HILL
40
22
Agat R.
Rio Gautali R.
Gautali R.
MT
ALIFAN
Maanot
Reservoir
MT
TAENE
MAANOT PASS
CONTOUR
1000

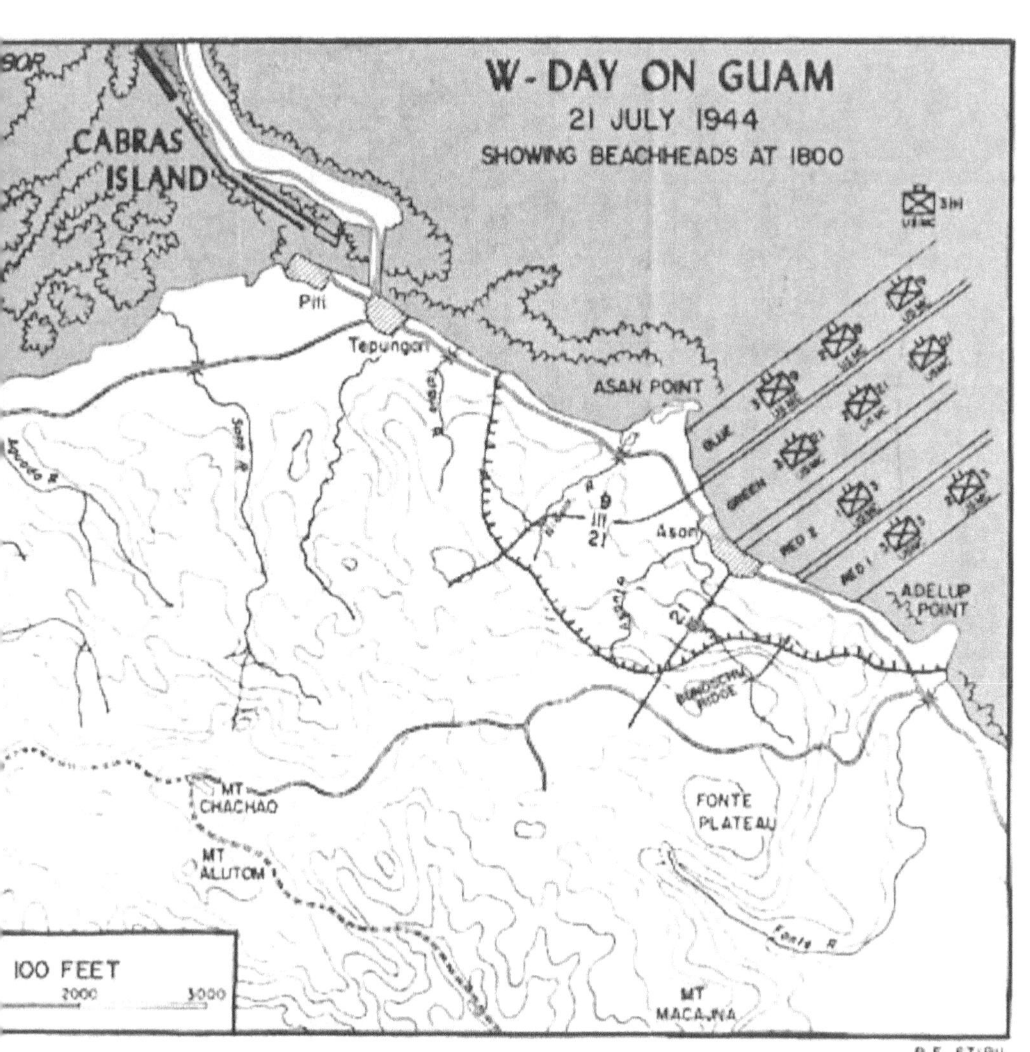

W-DAY ON GUAM
21 JULY 1944
SHOWING BEACHHEADS AT 1800
3 INF
USMC
CABRAS ISLAND
Pili
Tepungan
ASAN POINT
Asan
9
III
21
21
BLUE
GREEN
RED 2
RED 1
ADELUP POINT
BUNDSCHU RIDGE
MT CHACHAO
MT ALUTOM
FONTE PLATEAU
Fonte R
MT MACAJNA
100 FEET
2000
3000
R F STIBIL

W-DAY IN THE SOUTH

In the south, near Agat, in spite of a favorable terrain for the attack, the 1st Brigade, led by General Lemuel C. Shepherd, encountered intense enemy resistance at the beachhead. Much more than the 3rd Division found on the northern beaches. Japanese machine gun and small arms fire, along with two 75mm guns from a concrete blockhouse with a four-foot-thick roof, greeted the invading Marines as the LVTs churned ashore.

The blockhouse had been well camouflaged and not spotted before the landing as a bombing target. As a result, Japanese guns knocked out twenty-four amtracs carrying elements of the 22nd Marines. The W-Day assault forces' first hours on the southern beaches posed a major problem.

The Agat assault was given the same thunderous naval gunfire support, which disrupted and shook the ground before the landings on the northern beaches. When the 1st Brigade assault wave was less than a thousand yards from the beach, hundreds of 4.5-inch rockets from LCI(G)s (Landing Craft Infantry, Gunboat) slammed into the strand.

While the LCVPs, LVTs, and the DUKWs (amphibious trucks) were still offshore, there was virtually no enemy fire from the beach. Artillery observation planes reported no observed enemy fire. The defenders would respond in their own time. Because so many amtracs were lost as the assault waves neared the beaches, later in the day there would not be enough LVTs available for transferring men and supplies from boats to amtracs at Agat reef. The shortage of amphibious tractors would plague the brigade for days.

The precision of the Japanese guns caused severe damage to the cargo and assault craft on the beach. This became a real concern for General Shepherd. Most of the soldiers and some of the Marines who came in after the first assault waves waded ashore with full packs in waist high water. They faced the danger of both underwater shell holes and enemy fire. By the time the bulk of the 77th Division waded in, these twin threats were not as great because the Marines onshore were spread out and could keep the Japanese occupied.

The Japanese defenders prepared their defenses well—thick-walled bunkers and smaller pillboxes. On Gaan Point there were 75mm guns in the middle of the landing beaches. Crossfire from Gaan, coordinated with the machine guns on nearby Yona island, raked the beaches allocated to the 4th Marines. The 4th was tasked with establishing a beachhead and protecting the southernmost flank.

After vicious fighting, the 4th Marines advanced onto low ground and cleared Bangi Point where bunker walls could withstand a battleship round. The 4th Marines set up a road-block on Harmon Road leading down from the mountains to Agat. Previous operations had taught the Marines that the Japanese would be back in strength at night.

After the Marines landed, they found an under-manned but excellent Japanese trench system on the beaches. While the pre-landing bombardment had driven many defenders back into their holes, they poured heavy machine gun fire and mortar fire down on the invaders. The preinvasion planning called for the Marine amtracs to drive a thousand yards inland before disembarking Marines. This tactic failed because of a heavily mined beachhead and anti-tank ditches along with other obstacles.

But the Marines attacked with such overwhelming force that they broke through. And by 1030, the assault forces were over one-thousand yards inland. Now, the 4th Marines Reserve Battalion had finally landed after taking heavy fire from emplaced enemy forces. Marines worked on clearing bypassed bunkers using the now landed tanks. By 1320, the blockhouse on Gaan Point was eliminated by advancing to the rear and blasting the surprised enemy gunners before they could offer any resistance. By this time, General Shepherd was on the beach and had opened his command post.

The 22nd Marines were battered by a hail of small arms and mortar fire when they hit their assigned beach. They suffered heavy losses in equipment and men during the first few minutes. According to PFC William Dunlap, the battalion's beloved chaplain who had been entrusted with everyone's gambling money to "hold for safekeeping," had been killed. Marines never for a minute considered he was just as mortal as they were.

The 1/22 Marines left their section of the landing zone and advanced to the shattered town of a gap where the battalion drove north and eventually sealed off a heavily defended road to Orote Peninsula, soon to be the scene of a major battle.

The 2/22 Marines was in the center of the beachhead and hurried the 1,000 yards inland from the beach. The battalion could have taken one of its W-Day goals of securing the local heights of Mount Alifan—if American bombs and not fallen short and stalled their attack.

The 1st Battalion moved into the ruins of Agat and secured it by 1020. While there was still minor small arms resistance in the rubble, by 1130 the battalion was also out on Harmon Road leading to the northern shoulder of Mount Alifan. As the Marines advanced, Japanese shells hit the battalion aid station, wounding and killing several members of the medical team and destroying supplies. It wasn't until later that afternoon that the 1st Battalion finally received another doctor.

On the right flank of the landing waves, the 1/4 Marines ran head-on into Hill 40 near Bangi Point—which had been thoroughly hammered by the Navy. The unexpected fierce defense on Hill 40 demonstrated that the Japanese recognized its importance, commanding the beaches where troops and supplies came ashore. It took tanks and the support of the 3rd Battalion to secure that position.

The 2/22 Marines, before dark on W-Day, could see the 4th Marines from across a deep gully. The 4th held a twisted, thin line extending over 1,500 yards from the beach to Harmon Road, while the 22nd Marines held the rest of the beach at 5,000 yards long and 1,500 yards deep. General Shepherd summed it up to General Geiger on nightfall of W-Day: "casualties at about 350. Critical shortages of fuel and ammunition of all types. Enemy unknown. Think we can handle it. Will continue as planned tomorrow."

Support troops helped to ensure that Marines could stay on shore once they landed. The support troops struggled since daylight, trying to manage the flow of vital supplies to the beaches. As darkness on W-Day approached, a black unit, the 4th Ammunition Company, guarded the brigade's ammunition depot ashore. During a sleepless night, these black American

Marines killed fourteen enemy saboteurs sneaking into the ammo dump.

Poor communications delayed the order to land the Army's 305th Regimental Combat team for several hours. They were slated for a morning landing but there were no amtracs available, and the soldiers had to wade in from the reef. Some soldiers slipped underwater into shell holes and had to swim for their lives in high tide. When the rest of the 305th arrived on the beach, they were all soaked, and some were seasick.

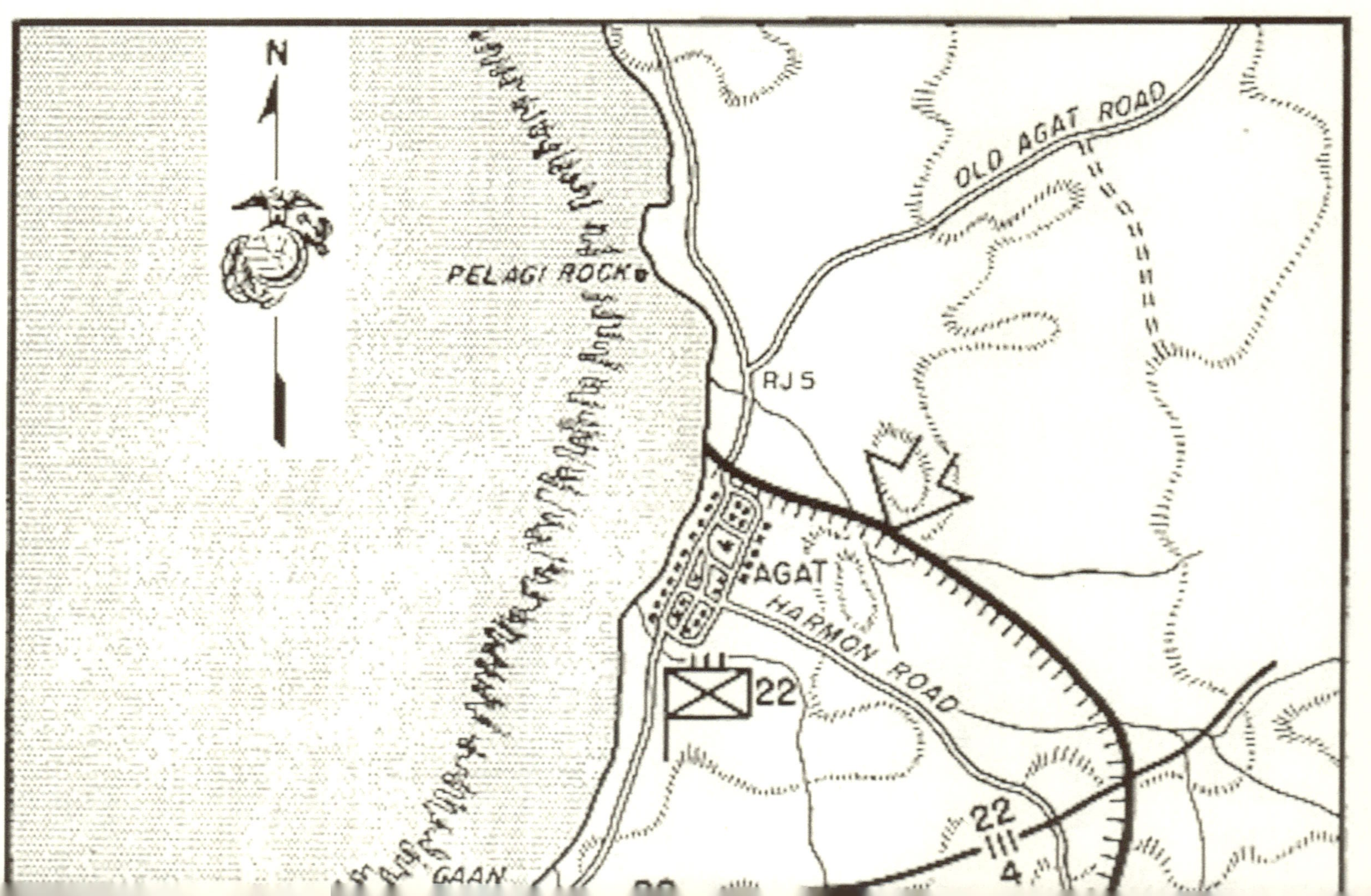

N
OLD AGAT ROAD
PELAGI ROCK
RJ 5
AGAT
HARMON ROAD
22
22
4
GAAN

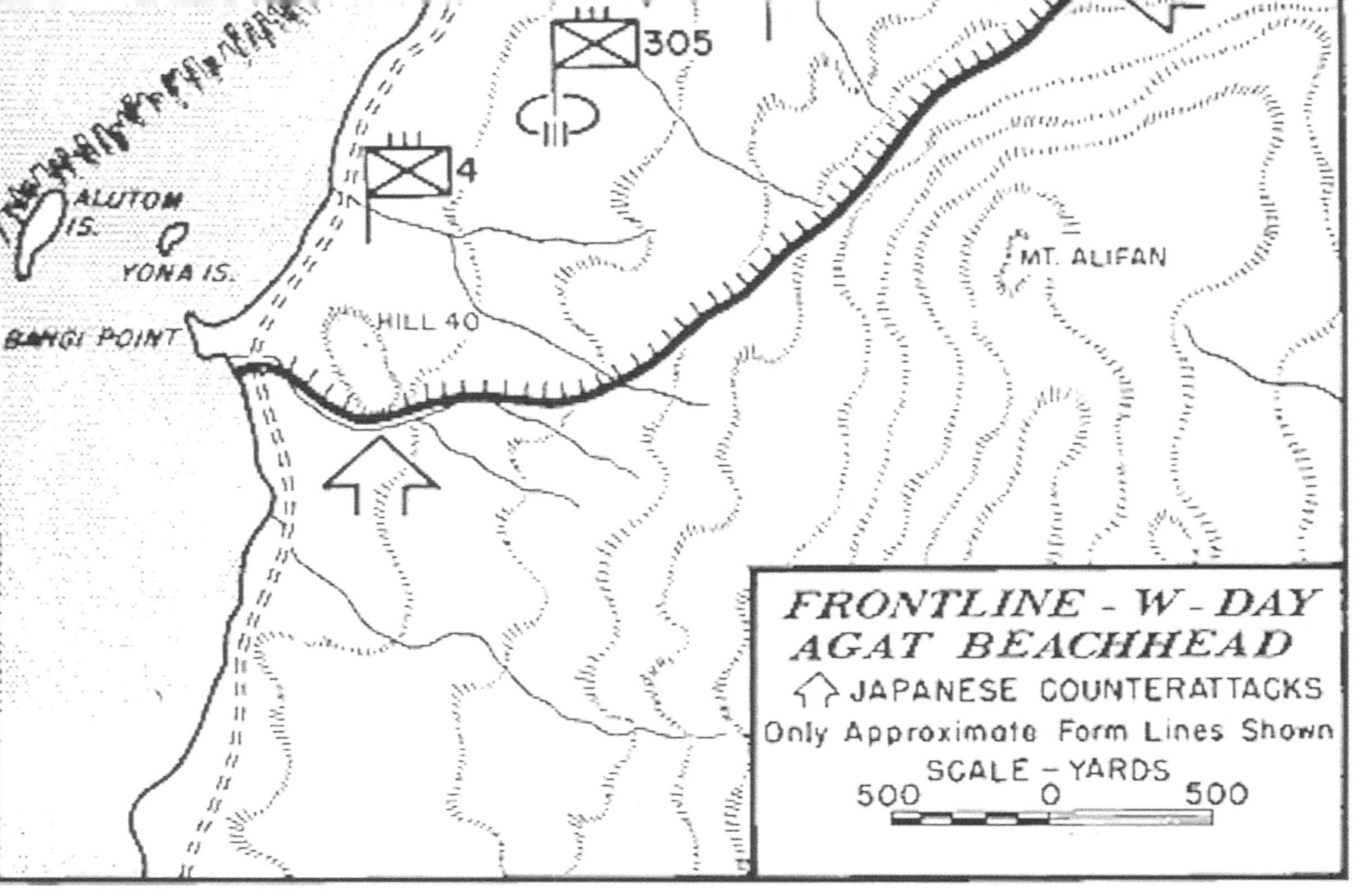
305
4
MT. ALIFAN
HILL 40
ALUTOM IS.
YONA IS.
BANGI POINT
FRONTLINE - W - DAY
AGAT BEACHHEAD
JAPANESE COUNTERATTACKS
Only Approximate Form Lines Shown
SCALE - YARDS
500   0   500

THE JAPANESE COUNTERATTACK

Colonel Suenaga commanded the *38th Regiment* from his command post on Mount Alifan. He watched the Americans overwhelm his forces below. Desperate to strike back, he called General Takashina and asked for permission for an all-out assault to drive the Marines back into the sea. He'd already ordered his remaining units to assemble for a counterattack. Takashina was not receptive at first. He said the losses would be too high and the *38th Regiment* would serve better defending the high ground and harassing the American advance.

Takashina did eventually give his permission and ordered any survivors to fall back on Mount Alifan if the attack failed —which he was certain it would. Colonel Suenaga must have shared the general's pessimism because he burned his regimental colors to prevent their capture before the counterattack.

The focal point of the Japanese attack came from the south on Hill 40. The brunt of the fighting would fall to the 3/4 Marines. A battalion of still mostly intact Japanese from the *38th Regiment* came north from reserve positions.

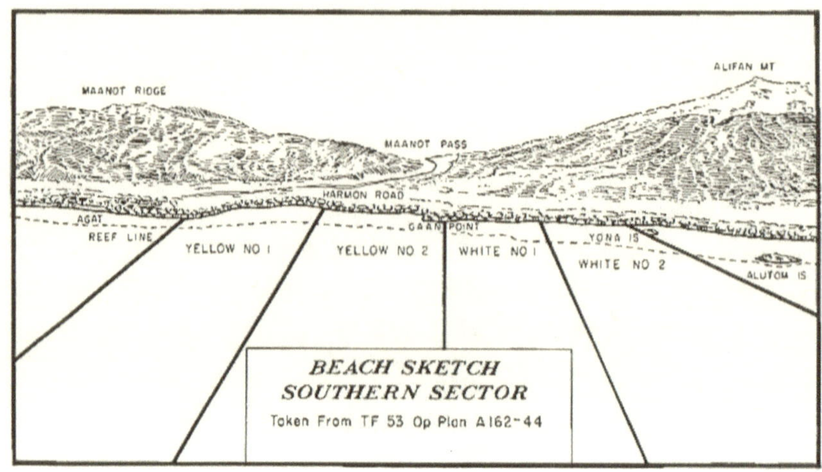

Lieutenant "Stormy" Sexton's Company K faced the brunt of the Japanese assault. Company K held, but barely. Sexton later wrote on that night's fighting: "if the Japs could've captured Hill 40, they would have kicked our asses off the Agat beaches."

The Japanese had 750 troops hit Company K at 2115 with their main thrust coming from the left or east of Hill 40.

According to Lieutenant Sexton: "They found a gap in our lines and overran the machine gun which covered the gap. The Japs broke through and advanced toward the beaches. Some elements turned left on Hill 40 and assaulted Company K from the rear. We fought them all night long with our 200 men from Hill 40 and a small hill to the rear and northeast. At daylight, Marines counterattacked with two squads and two tanks closing the gap. Many of our men from Company K died that night. All 750 Jap soldiers were destroyed. That hill symbolized the whole hard-fought American victory on Guam.

"All along the rest of the Marine front, and the reserve areas, the fighting was hot and heavy as the rest of the *38th* attacked. Colonel Suenaga pushed his troops to attack again and again. In the light of our flares, I watched them get mowed down from machine gun fire. General Shepherd was no novice to Jap tactics. He'd expected this attack and was ready for them.

"Jap reconnaissance patrols were numerous and around 2130 they tried to draw our fire and determine our positions. Suenaga was out in front of the center thrust, which began at 2315 after a brisk mortar flurry on the right flank of the 4th Marines. The enemy advanced in full force, charging with rifles carried at high port, yelling, and throwing grenades. Marines lurked in the dark shadows and moved across the skyline under the light of stars from the ships. Marines lined up hand grenades, waited, watched, and then reacted.

"Japs were everywhere trying to bayonet Marines in their foxholes. They even got down to the pack howitzer positions in the rear of the front lines. It was the same for the 22nd Marines. A whole company of Japs got close to the regimental command post. The defense was held largely by a reconnaissance platoon led by Lieutenant Dennis Chavez, who killed five Japs at point-blank range with a Thompson submachine gun.

"Six enemy tanks lumbered down Harmon Road. They were met by bazooka men. Private First Class Bruno Oribiletti knocked out the first two enemy tanks before Marine Shermans from the 4th Tank Company finished off the rest. Oribiletti was killed but was posthumously awarded the Navy Cross for his bravery.

"Enemy troops from the *38th* also stumbled into the perimeter of the newly arrived 305th Infantry and paid for it with their lives."

After a night and a day of furious battle, the *38th* ceased to exist. Colonel Suenaga, wounded in the first night's counterattack, continued to flail at the Marines until he also was cut down. Takashina ordered the shattered remnants of the regiment north to join the reserves he'd need to defend the high ground around Fonte Ridge above the beachhead. Here, the general would leave his troops to fend for themselves.

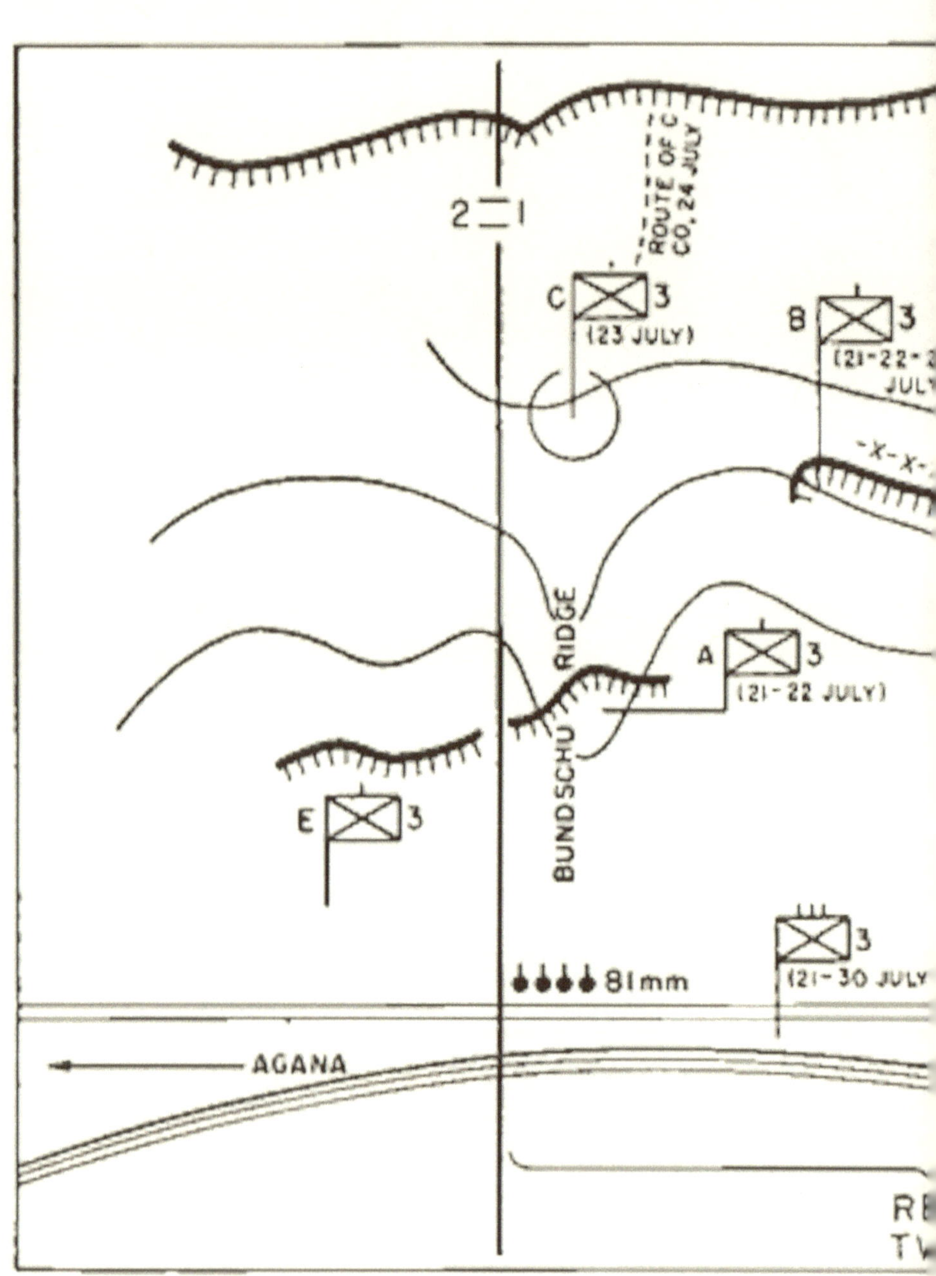

2 — 1
ROUTE OF C
CO, 24 JULY
C 3
(23 JULY)
B 3
(21-22-2
JUL
-X-X-
A 3
(21-22 JULY)
BUNDSCHU RIDGE
E 3
3
(21-30 JULY
81mm
AGANA
R
TV

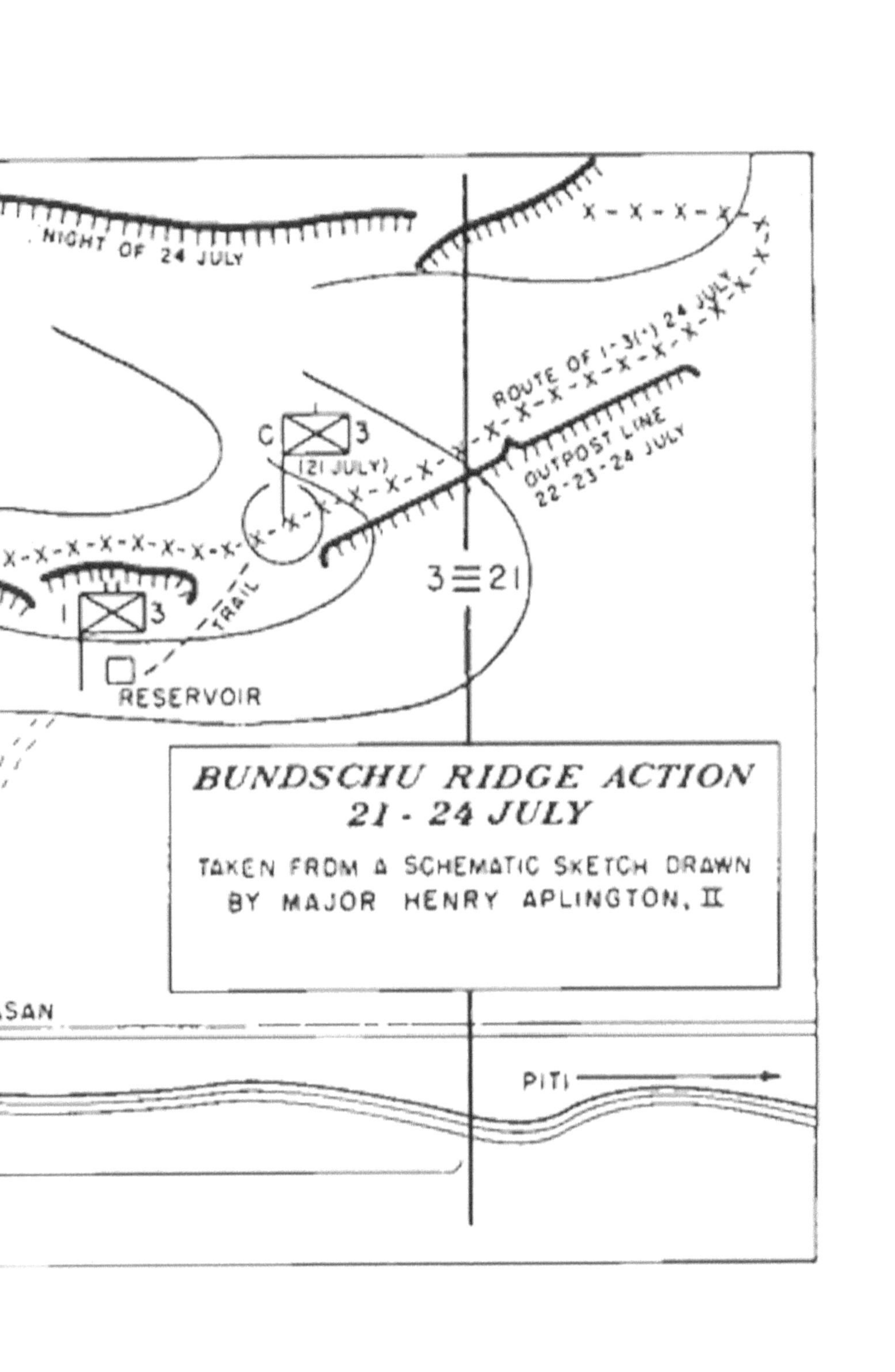

BUNDSCHU RIDGE ACTION
21 - 24 JULY

TAKEN FROM A SCHEMATIC SKETCH DRAWN
BY MAJOR HENRY APLINGTON, II

BATTLE OF FONTE RIDGE

After two days of fierce fighting on the left flank of the 3rd Division Marines' beachhead, in an area now known as Bundschu Ridge, the Marines suffered 613 casualties.

The 21st Marines, in the center, delayed their advance on July 22 until the 3rd could catch up. Marines in exposed ridge positions were getting hammered by Japanese mortar fire. The barrage was so intense that Colonel Arthur H. Butler, in charge of the regiment, called up the division reserve to replace the 1st Battalion with the 2nd.

The 9th Marines encountered little resistance while overrunning several abandoned Japanese positions in its drive to the shores of Apra Harbor. The 3rd Battalion, with the support of naval gunfire and bombs, assaulted Cabras Island. Marines landing in LVTs found hundreds of mines hidden in dense brambles.

General Turnage assessed the situation on July 22 and wrote: "Japanese resistance increased considerably today on the division's left and center. All of 3rd Battalion's combat team were committed to a continuous attack since landing.

The 21st CT [combat team] has been relieved by division reserve. Former is forty percent depleted. Any further advance will continue to thin our lines. It is now apparent that an additional combat team is needed. The 9th is fully committed to the capture of Cabras and Piti. Urgently recommend an additional combat team be attached to this division at the earliest possible time."

Turnage was refused the additional combat team he sought. The night of W+1 was fairly quiet in the 3rd Division's sector. Except for the 1/21 Marines, who repulsed a Japanese counterattack complete with a mortar barrage and followed by a bayonet charge.

The III Amphibious Corps commander, General Geiger, was aware that most Japanese troops had not yet been encountered. He told the 3rd Division: "close contact between adjacent units needed to become established by late afternoon and maintained throughout the night."

Despite orders to close gaps and keep contact, the 3rd Division was spread too thin to hold. When they halted for the night, they realized the distance between the units had widened. As night fell, front-line troops held strong points with gaps between them covered by interlocking bands of fire.

The 3rd Marines reached the high ground of Bundschu Ridge on the 23rd. They hunted the remaining enemy stragglers. The enemy had withdrawn from the immediate area but hadn't gone far. When the 21st Marines' patrols tried to link up with the 3rd Marines, they were pushed back by fire from cleverly hidden machine guns. Nearly impossible to spot in the underground and rock-strewn ravines. All along the ridges that the Marines held were stretches of deadly open ground that completely blanketed enemy fire from higher positions.

On the night of the 23rd, the 9th Marines advanced through open territory dotted by hills, each of which a potential enemy bastion. Patrols sent south along the shoreline to contact the 1st Brigade took fire from the hills on its left flank. They also ran into a concentration of American artillery and naval gunfire directed at the enemy defenders on Orote. The patrol was permitted to turn back.

On the 24th, the 3rd and 21st Marine Regiments finally made contact on the heights. But the linkup was an illusion. There were no solid front lines, only strong points. No one could be certain that the Japanese had all been accounted for. But the areas that had been probed and attacked now seemed secure.

Every rifleman knew that much of the same lay ahead. They saw their next objective on the horizon to the front on the Mount Tenjo Road that crossed the high ground, framing the beachhead.

The division had already suffered over 2,000 casualties—the majority in the infantry units. The Japanese, who'd lost just as many if not more men in the north alone, showed no signs of abandoning their ferocious defense. General Takashina gathered his forces to prepare an all-out counterattack as Marines were advancing to their first objective on the FBHL (Force Beachhead Line), securing the high ground and linking up the two beachheads.

Takashina had been bringing his reserve troops into the rugged hills along Mount Tenjo Road since the American landings. He called in his reserves from scattered positions all over the island. By July 25, W-Day+4, he had over 5,000 men, mostly made up of the *10th Independent Mixed Regiment,* in position and ready to attack.

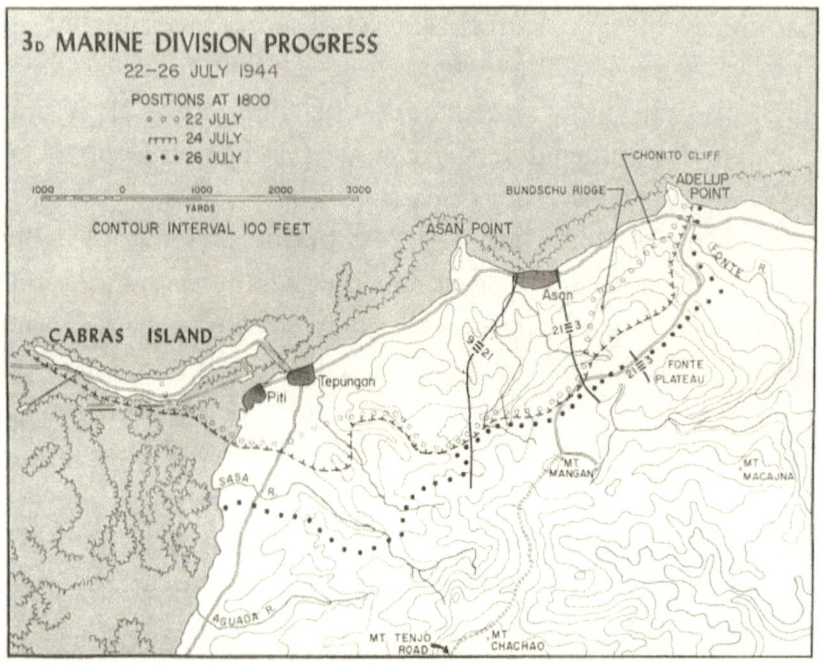

The fighting on the 25th was as intense as any since the
Marines invaded. The 2/9 Marines were attached to the 3rd
Marines to bring a relatively intact unit into the fight and give
the battered 1/3 Marines a chance to recover. By nightfall, the
2/9 Marines had driven a wedge into the Japanese lines and
took Mount Tenjo Road. They were only four hundred yards
short of reaching their objective at Fonte.

Throughout the relentless firefights, the 3rd Marines
blasted and burned their way through barriers of enemy cave
defenses. They finally linked up with the 9th Marines on the
left. At 1900, Company G of 9th Marines pulled back one
hundred yards to position themselves forward of the road,
giving them a better observation wind field of fire. Company F
reached an occupied rocky prominence some one hundred
fifty yards ahead of Company G in the center while they also
pulled back for a better defense. The scene was set for a

pitched battle on Fonte Ridge. Captain Louis Wilson (who became the 26th Commandant of the Marine Corps in 1976) led Company F in the intense fight for Fonte Ridge in which casualties were caused on both sides from small arms fire at point-blank range.

Captain Wilson was awarded the Medal of Honor for his leadership, doggedness, and organizational skill under fire. Wilson was wounded three times while he led attacks into the core of the Fonte action. Part of his citation reads: "In fierce fighting and hand-to-hand encounters, he led his men in a furiously waged battle for ten hours and tenaciously held his line and repelled fanatic counterattacks from the Japanese until he crushed the last efforts of the hard-pressed enemy."

Captain Wilson led and organized the seventeen-man patrol that climbed the slope in the face of the continuous enemy fire, seizing Fonte's critical high ground.

Colonel Frazier West recalled the battle for Fonte Ridge as brisk, bitter, and close. A young officer, West commanded Company G and reinforced Wilson's unit. He joined Company F's flank and then reconnoitered to spot enemy positions and shared the night in a joint command post with Captain Wilson.

In late afternoon on the 25th, a platoon of four tanks from Company C made their way up Mount Tenjo Road and got into position facing the Japanese strongpoints. At the climax of the battle, Wilson and West's companies were still holding their positions. First Lieutenant Wilcie O'Bannon, the XO of Company F, got downslope from his exposed position and brought up two tanks. By using telephones mounted in the rear of these tanks to communicate with the Marines inside, O'Bannon described targets for the tanks as he positioned them to support West's and Wilson's Marines.

The tanks came up with the precious cargo of ammunition. Volunteers stuffed grenades in their pockets and hung bandoleers over shoulders, pocketed clips, and carried grenade boxes on their shoulders to deliver like birthday presents all along the line to Companies F and G—and what was left of Company E.

Colonel West used a tank radio circuit to call in naval gunfire. This guaranteed that all the terrain before him would be lit all night by star shells and high explosive naval gunfire.

At dawn on July 26, over 600 dead Japanese laid in front of the 2/9 Marine positions. But the battle was not over. General Turnage ordered the crest of the reverse slope taken. More Japanese counterattacks would come, and again fighting would be hand-to-hand. But by July 28, the capture of Fonte Ridge was no longer in question. Companies E, F, and G took their objectives on the crest, costing the battalion 242 casualties in four murderous days.

The 21st Marines did not have it any easier on the 25th. After a hard morning of fighting, they were able to clear the front in the center of the line. The 2/21 Marines dealt with similar pockets of diehard enemy soldiers like those that held up the 2/9 Marines on Fonte. Hidden in cave positions on the eastern draw of the Asan River, inland from the beachhead.

The Japanese were destroyed only after repeated Marine assaults and close-in fighting. According to the official Marine Corps history of the campaign: "every foot of ground that fell to the Marines were paid in heavy casualties, and every man available was needed in the assault."

The 9th Marines made good progress on the 25th and reached their objective of the Sasa River by 0915. The 9th Marines had even taken more ground than was planned. From there, General Turnage repositioned the 9th Marines to support the fighting on the struggling left flank. The 2nd Battalion pulled out of position to reinforce the 3rd Marines, and the remaining two battalions spread out a little further in their position.

A determined enemy counterattack hit the 3rd Division Marines on the night of July 25. The intensity of the Japanese counterattack was matched across the 3rd Division's front. It wasn't long before Japanese troops roaming the rear slipped into Marine perimeters and snuck downstream into valleys and ravines leading to the beaches.

Major Henry Aplington II commanded the 1/3 Marines, the only infantry reserve. His Marines held positions on the hills of what had been a quiet sector. He wrote: "Heavy rain came when it got dark. On the line, Marines huddled under ponchos in their wet foxholes, trying to figure out the meaning of the obvious activity by the Japanese.

"Near midnight the Japs were probing the 21st Marines' lines and slopping over into those of the 9th Marines. All was quiet in our circle of hills, and we received no notifications when the probing increased its intensity or at 0400 when the enemy opened their attack. My first inkling came at about 0430 when my three companies on the hills erupted into fire and called for mortar support. I talked to the company commanders and asked them what was going on, only to be told that the Japs were all around them. The enemy was close. Three of my dead had been killed by bayonet attacks."

Private Dale Fetzer was a dog handler assigned to the 1/9 Marines with his black Labrador Retriever. His dog Skipper was asleep in front of his handler's foxhole. Suddenly Skipper bolted upright. His nose pointed up and toward Mount Tenjo. Private Fetzer shouted, "get the lieutenant. The Japs are coming."

Japanese troops poured down the slopes at 0400 in a furious banzai attack. The enemy had been sighted drinking during the afternoon in the higher hills and now some appeared drunk.

The 21st Marines were along a low ridge close to Mount Tenjo Road. The banzai charge smashed against the 3rd Battalion, and the enemy seized a machine gun position—quickly recaptured by Marines. The 3rd Division held a thin front on the right flank of the 21st Marines and to the left of the 9th Marines.

Some of the Japanese raiders got through the sparsely manned gap between the battalions. The Japanese charged fearlessly at the artillery, tanks, and ammunition supply dumps. Their attack was scattered and unorganized. But fighting was brutal and shattered the hastily erected Marine roadblock between the battalions.

Some attackers got through the lines along the front. Fifty enemy troops reached the division hospital. Doctors evacuated the gravely wounded, but the walking wounded joined stretcher-bearers, cooks, bakers, and corpsmen to form a line fighting off the attackers. One of the walking wounded, Private Michael Ryan, ran with a wounded foot through cross-fire to join the line and help fight off the enemy assault.

Colonel George Van Orden assembled two companies of the 3rd Pioneer Battalion to eliminate this threat. Marine pioneers killed thirty-three enemy troops in less than three hours and only lost three of their men. The 3rd Medical Battalion took twenty casualties, but only one patient was killed in the fighting.

For many men in this furious and confused melee breaking out over Marine positions, Corporal Charles Moore's experiences weren't unique. His outfit held a position along a quarter mile from Fonte plateau. He later wrote: "We set up on the road that made a sharp turn overlooking a draw. It was Second Platoon's last stand. Three attacks that night, and by the third, no one was left to fight—so they broke through. They came in droves, throwing hand grenades and hacked up some of our platoon. In the morning, I only had ten rounds of ammo left and half the clip for my BAR. I was holding those rounds back in case I needed them to make a break for it. Everyone was quiet, either wounded or dead. The Japs came in to take out their dead and wounded steps from the edge of my foxhole. I held my breath. I watched them as they milled around until dawn, and then they left."

With the seizure of Fonte Ridge, the capture of the beachhead was now complete. The 3rd Division fought bravely throughout the bloody night until they finished off the determined Japanese enemy on Guam. What made the fighting for Fonte important was the fact that the advance to the north end of the island could not take place until Fonte Ridge was seized and held.

The enemy attack also failed in the south, although it was touch and go at times. However, Japanese sailors on Orote were just as committed as the soldiers on Fonte to drive the Allies from Guam.

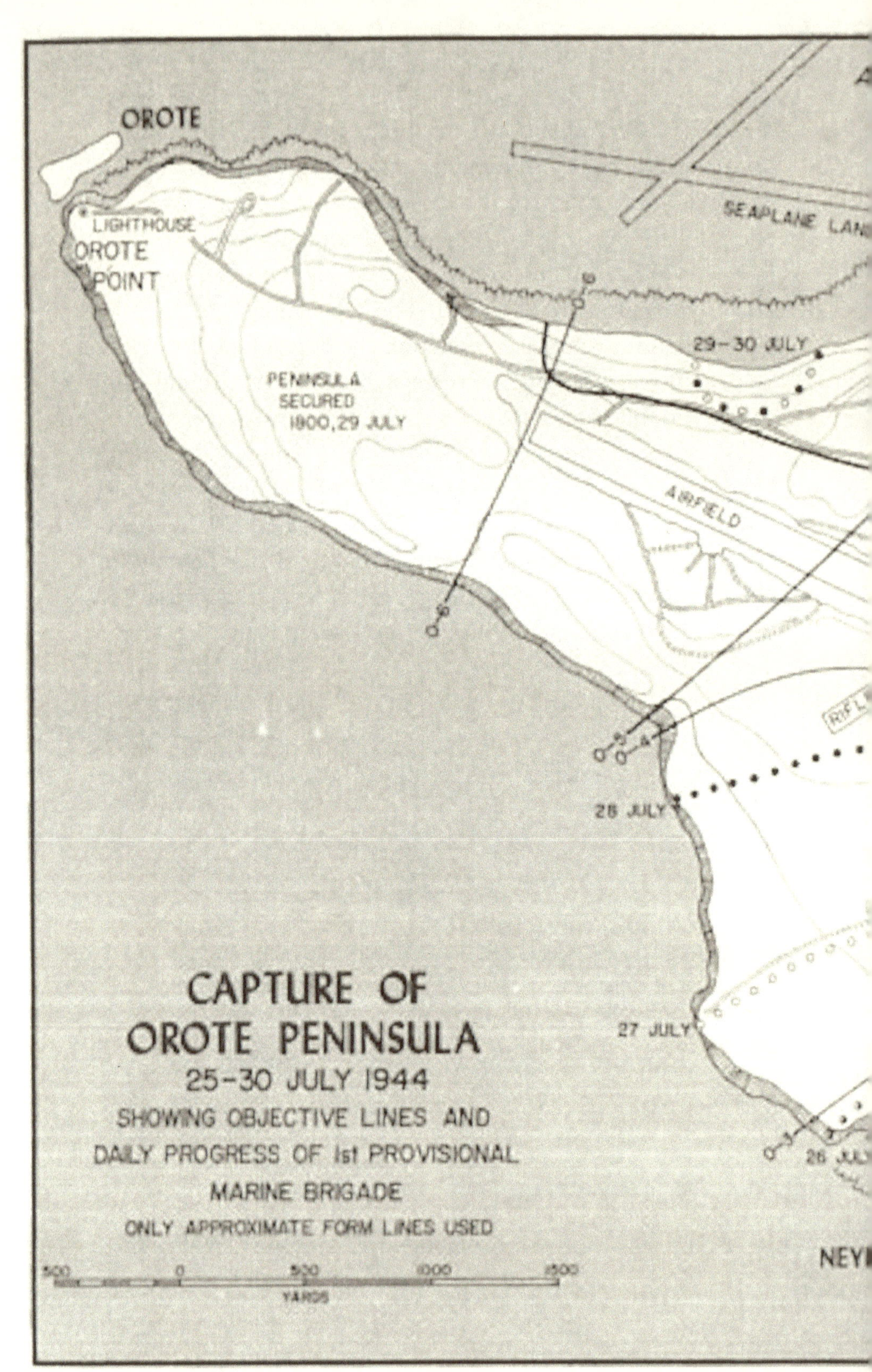

OROTE
LIGHTHOUSE
OROTE
POINT
PENINSULA
SECURED
1800, 29 JULY
SEAPLANE LAN
29-30 JULY
AIRFIELD
RIFL
28 JULY
27 JULY
26 JUL
NEY
CAPTURE OF
OROTE PENINSULA
25-30 JULY 1944
SHOWING OBJECTIVE LINES AND
DAILY PROGRESS OF 1st PROVISIONAL
MARINE BRIGADE
ONLY APPROXIMATE FORM LINES USED
500   0   500   1000   1500
YARDS

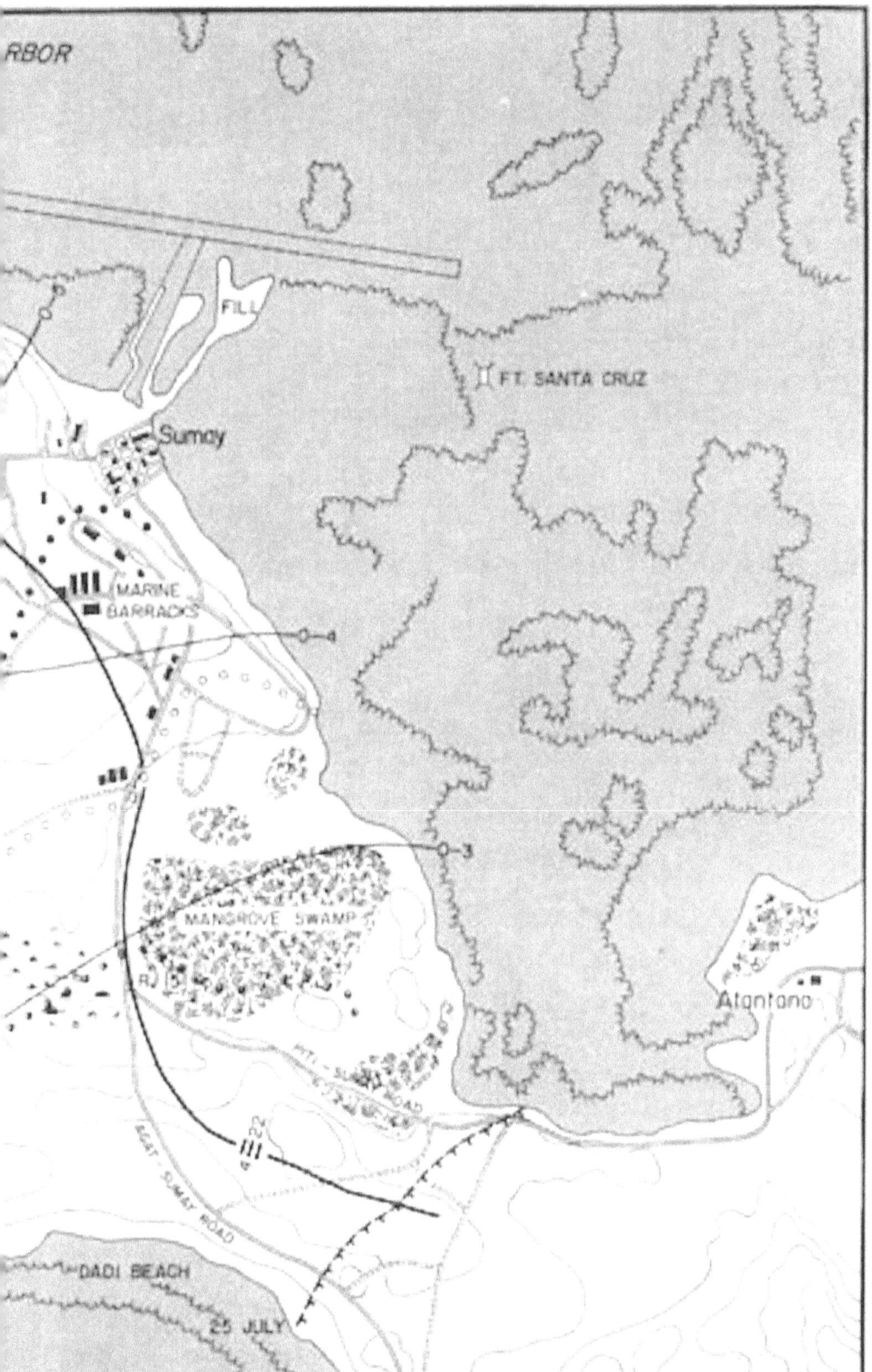
RBOR
FILL
FT. SANTA CRUZ
Sumay
MARINE
BARRACKS
4
3
MANGROVE SWAMP
Atantano
22
FLOAT-SUMAY ROAD
DADI BEACH
25 JULY

CAPTURE OF OROTE PENINSULA

The 22nd Marines advanced up the coast from Agat and fought a series of brutal battles against stubborn enemy defenders. The 4th Marines swept up the slopes of Mount Alifan and secured the high ground overlooking the beachhead. By the 25th, the brigade lined up across from the mouth of the Orote Peninsula. They faced formidable Japanese defenses. Enemy defenders were anchored in swamps and low hillocks concealed by heavy undergrowth—bristling with automatic weapons.

The 77th Infantry Division took over the rest of the southern beachhead, relieving the 4th Marines of their patrolling duties in the hills to the west. Artillery and naval guns pounded the Japanese on Orote without letup. In case of an enemy air attack, beach defenses from Bangi Point to Agat were manned by the 9th Defense Battalion. Few Japanese planes were still in the sky, so antiaircraft gunners concentrated their firing across the water into the southern flank of enemy positions on Orote.

The 14th Defense Battalion on Cabras Island moved into position to provide direct flanking fire on the Peninsula's northern coast. They stood ready to elevate their guns and fire at enemy planes in the skies.

At dawn on July 26, over 5,000 Japanese troops on Orote took part in General Takashina's desperate counterattack. Enemy soldiers stormed out of the mangrove swamp and charged with swords, grenades, and small arms fire. Like in the north, many of the Japanese attackers had fortified themselves with *sake*. Japanese officers led senseless soldiers who attacked Marine tanks armed only with samurai swords. There were also skilled and deadly attacks. Marines were stabbed and sliced in their foxholes.

In charge of Company L of the 22nd Marines, Captain Robert Frank was on the front relaying enemy positions to brigade artillery. He later wrote: "The artillery response was effective and intense. The fire was drawn in closer to our front lines. We threw over 25,000 shells into the pockets of the Japanese between midnight and 3 AM. Screaming banzai attacks came at 1230 and then again at 0145 and 0315. At daylight, muddy ground in front of Marine positions was slick with blood. Over 400 Japanese bodies were sprawled out in the driving rain."

General Shepherd knew his front-line troops, the 4th Marines on the left and 22nd Marines on the right, could withstand the night's banzai attacks. He ordered a counterattack launched at 0730. But first, there would be another artillery barrage. At dawn, the bombardment opened with the 77th Infantry Division's 105s and 155s, and whatever other guns the 12th Marines could spare. This became one of the most intense barrages of the campaign.

Major Charles Davis of the 77th Division Artillery later wrote about General Shepherd's request to turn the heavy guns to face Orote in order to soften Japanese positions. The 105s and 155s hammered the enemy defenders' well-prepared positions and shredded the protection, covering, and camouflage from bunkers and trenches. Pieces of Japanese troops hung in trees. Marines saw that this fire was effective and made it a point to return and congratulate the section leaders from the 77th Artillery.

When the advance came, it only moved one hundred yards before it was attacked by a blistering front of machine gun and small arms fire. Enemy artillery fell furiously, leaving Marines wondering if the fire was from their own guns—a favorite Japanese tactic. The Japanese return fire stalled the 22nd Marine's advance. It wasn't until 0830 before the attack was in full force again, spearheaded by Army tanks.

In front of the 22nd Marines was that mangrove swamp where the banzai attack was mounted the night before. Still heavily occupied by the Japanese, the only way to penetrate it was through a 200-yard-long corridor along the regimental boundary covered by Japanese fire. It could only be navigated under cover of tanks. Armor gunners and commanders directed their fire just over the head of prone Marines into the gun ports of enemy pillboxes.

By 1250, Marines had worked their way through the bottlenecks and passed the mangrove swamps—destroying bunkers with flamethrowers and demolitions. The 4th Marines' assault battalions kept pace with this advance and found it somewhat easier terrain, but the defenders were just as determined. By evening, the brigade advanced 1,100 yards from its jump-off line. Both regiments were weary and dug in with an all-around defense.

After a massive pre-attack barrage on the 27th, Marines were stalled again before they'd gone a hundred yards. The 3/4 Marines were up against a well-defended ridge, a sinister clearing, and a coconut grove. This ridge was close to the tactically essential goals of the old Marine barracks, its rifle range, and the Orote Airfield runways. With heavy tank support, the 22nd Marines surged past their initial obstacles, and by midafternoon, they reached positions well beyond the morning's battles.

On the left flank, the 4th Marines faced a lighter resistance. They were led by tanks that knocked down the brush. Colonel Samuel Puller, brother of the famous Colonel "Chesty" Puller, was killed by a sniper.

By early afternoon, assault elements of the 4th Marines broke out of the grove short of the rifle range. They were stalled by enemy dug-in defenses and minefields. A Japanese officer emerged and brandished his sword at a tank. Not an unusual sight in the climax of this losing engagement. This was easier than a ritual suicide.

The horror of the American guns must've been too much for the enemy defenders on the immediate front. They cut and ran from their strong and well-defended positions. Marines didn't care why the enemy ran—just that they ran—and dug in less than 300 yards from the prized target. This squeezed the enemy into the last quadrant of the peninsula. All their entrenched defenses failed to hold. The Orote Airfield, old Marine barracks, and old parade ground, which hadn't seen American boots since December 10, 1941, were recaptured.

On July 28, General Shepherd ordered an all-out barrage of the Japanese naval defenders: a thirty-minute naval gunfire bombardment, a forty-five-minute airstrike, joined by whatever guns the brigade, 77th Division, and any antiaircraft battalions could muster. At 0830, the brigade launched an attack to retake Orote Airfield.

The 22nd Marines would assault the barracks, while the 4th Marines would advance on the airfield and rifle range. Japanese mortar fire and artillery had lessened, but small arms and machine guns were still intense when the Marines attacked. To the bitter end, Japanese defenders evoked a last-ditch stubbornness. American tanks were called up, but most had problems with control and visibility. Wherever there was a thick scrub brush, the enemy was concealed.

General Shepherd wanted this battle over. He ordered a massive infantry and tank advance jumping off at 1530 on the

28th. The Japanese refused to quit: it was do or die. By night-fall, the objectives were in sight, but there were still a few hundred yards to gain. Marines dug in for the night and hoped the Japanese would sacrifice themselves in another counterat-tack—no such luck.

The next day, the attack resumed. After the usual artillery barrage and heavy airstrikes, Marine and Army tanks led the way onto the airfield. Resistance was meager. By early after-noon, the airfield was secured. The 22nd Marines occupied what was left of the old Marine barracks. A bronze plaque, once mounted mounted on the barracks entrance, but now removed, was recovered and put up for reinstallation at a future date.

The Japanese found this latest advance too hard to accept. Suicides were random and many enemy soldiers jumped off cliffs, cut their own throats, and hugged exploding grenades.

Private First Class George Eftang watched several enemy suicides and later wrote: "I watched the Japanese jump to their deaths. I actually felt sorry for them. I knew they had families and sweethearts just like anyone else."

While the peninsula still swarmed with patrols, Generals Geiger, Larson, Shepherd, Admiral Spruance, and others who could be spared, took part in a ceremonial flag-raising and heartfelt tribute to an old barracks and those Marines who'd made it home. General Geiger called it hallowed ground and told those assembled, a hastily cleaned up honor guard of brigade troops: "you've avenged the loss of our comrades who were overcome by a numerically superior force three days after Pearl Harbor. Under our flag, this island again stands ready to fulfill its destiny as an American fortress in the Pacific."

Many of the Marines taking part in the ceremony could only thank God that they were still alive. At the end of the ceremony, engineers moved on to the airfield and filled many of the bomb and shell holes. Just six hours after the first bull-dozer had clanked out onto the runway, a navy torpedo bomber made an emergency landing. Soon after, light artillery spotting planes flew in regularly. The capture of the Orote Peninsula cost the brigade 874 casualties, with 115 men killed. Japanese dead was a staggering 1,633. On Orote, like Fonte, many enemy troops were still unaccounted for and likely ready to fight to prevent the capture of the island.

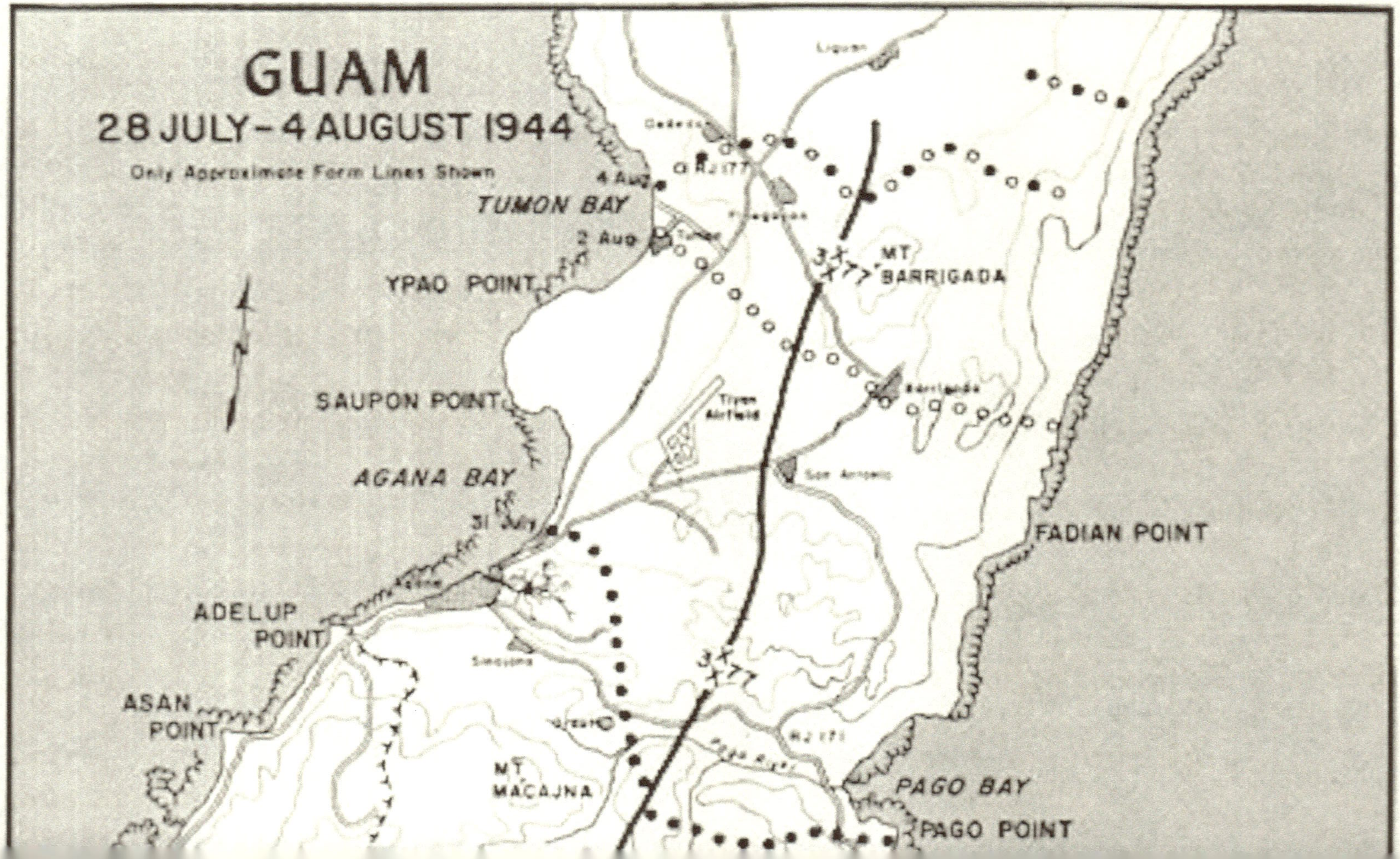

GUAM
28 JULY – 4 AUGUST 1944
Only Approximate Form Lines Shown
TUMON BAY
4 Aug
2 Aug
YPAO POINT
SAUPON POINT
AGANA BAY
31 July
ADELUP POINT
ASAN POINT
MT MACAJNA
Liguan
R J 177
MT BARRIGADA
3 X 177
Tiyan Airfield
Barrigada
San Antonio
3 X 177
Sinajana
R J 171
Pago River
FADIAN POINT
PAGO BAY
PAGO POINT

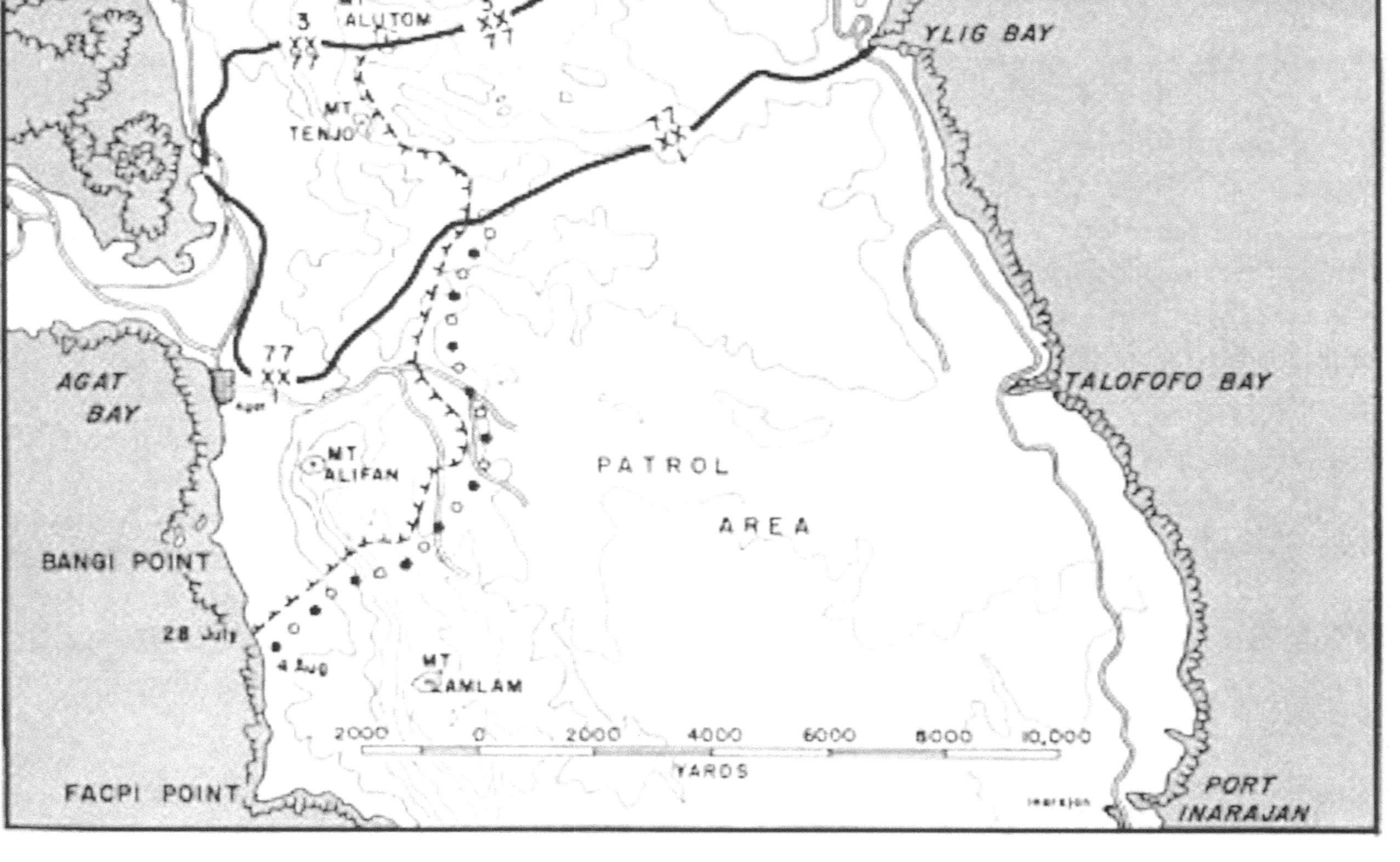

3 ALUTOM
XX 77
XX 77
MT TENJO
77 XX
77 XX
YLIG BAY
AGAT BAY
TALOFOFO BAY
MT ALIFAN
BANGI POINT
28 July
4 Aug
MT LAMLAM
PATROL AREA
2000 0 2000 4000 6000 8000 10,000
YARDS
FACPI POINT
PORT INARAJAN

TURNING POINT ON GUAM

After the breakthrough at Fonte and the failure of General Takashina's counterattack, American positions could now be consolidated. The 3rd and 21st Marines tightened their grasp on the heights, while the 9th Marines advanced up to Mount Chachao and Mount Alutom.

Across the hills at the base of Mount Chachao was the fiercest resistance. Major Donald Hubbard, in charge of the 3/9 Marines, called down artillery, and after the barrages, Marines attacked with bayonets and grenades. They destroyed everything that stood in their way. When the fight was over, Major Hubbard's Battalion counted over 130 dead Japanese. As their assault force pushed up the slopes, Marines spotted men from Company A of the 305th Infantry on top of Mount Tenjo to the west. Mount Tenjo had initially been in the 3rd Division's zone, but command wanted to get men on high ground so they could push ahead along the heights and not get trapped in ravines.

Japanese dead from the counterattack was 3,200. The destruction of General Takashina's infantry officers was estimated at 96%. Takashina himself was killed from a machine gun on an American tank as he urged survivors out of the Fonte position and on to the north to fight again. After Takashina's death, the tactical command of all Japanese forces on Guam was assumed by General Obata. He only had a handful of senior officers remaining to rally the Japanese defenders and organize a cohesive unit from the battalions' destroyed remnants.

On the night of July 28, Obata's defenders trudged along the path that led from Ordot to Fonte. They found their way by the light of the American flares. Two traffic control points guided men toward Barrigada, where three infantry companies were forming. General Obata fully expected the Americans to engage in an aggressive pursuit on the 29th. Obata organized a delaying force to hold back Marines until the Japanese withdrawal could be made.

General Geiger instead decided to rest his battle-weary troops before launching another full-scale attack to the north. His orders to the 3rd and 77th Divisions on July 29 were to eliminate any Japanese resistance and organize a line of defense and patrol in strength to the front. By capturing the beachhead line and its critical high ground, they were able to annihilate great numbers of Japanese—the turning point on Guam had finally been reached.

Still, the few enemy who'd surrendered, and those captured were wounded, dazed or unable to resist. Nearly all the enemy died fighting. Even when their lives were lost without purpose or sense. Yet, a substantial number of troops from the *29th Division* were not accounted for. General Geiger's intelligence sections estimated only one-quarter of the island's enemy troop strength had been on the island. He needed to make sure his rear was secure from attack before chasing north after the enemy. Captured Japanese prisoners, documents, and sightings from aircraft indicated to Geiger that the Japanese had withdrawn north to better roads. The north was denser and had a more concealing jungle—a better terrain for strong points.

General Geiger had the 77th Division scour Guam's southern half to ensure his rear was not threatened. He intensified and repeated the searches the brigade had made. Soldiers like the Marines before them found native Guamanians everywhere—some on farms and ranches and others in Japanese camps.

The natives were surprised to see Americans so soon after the landings and reported only small Japanese bands, usually only single soldiers. It became clear to Geiger that the combat units remaining were in the north and not the south. Best estimates of enemy strength were around 6,000 men.

General Obata expected a swift pursuit and set up a strong rearguard to give his retreating forces time to organize. While victory was no longer even a dream, the Japanese could still extract a painful cost. Geiger moved his troops back into attack positions across the width of the island. Frequent strong patrols were sent out to find cross-country routes and clues of enemy strength and dispositions.

General Obata organized a delaying defensive on the south slopes of Mount Barrigada and into the little town of Barrigada itself—only twenty houses. On all the approaches to the final defensive positions in the northwest corner of the island, Obata organized roadblocks at trail and road junctions. He concealed troops in the jungle to interdict the roads that were the only practical approach route to the northern end of the island.

General Obata felt overwhelmed as he later revealed in his notes: "the enemy air force seeks out our units during daylight hours in the forest and will bomb and strafe even a single soldier."

Even more damaging than the air attacks were the continuous naval gunfire and artillery bombardments brought down on men, guns, and trenches, by Army spotter planes—constantly patrolling overhead.

THE NORTHERN ASSAULT

General Geiger knew the probable route of the Japanese retreat. He drew up a list of objectives across the island to seize all the enemy's strong points.

The jump-off for this drive north was 0630 on July 31. The 3rd Marine Division would be on the left, the 77th Infantry Division on the right—splitting the island down the middle. Marine zones would include the island capital of Agana, enemy airfields at Finegayan, Tiyan, and Tumon Bay's beachhead.

The 77th took Mount Santa Rosa, Mount Barrigada, and Yigo. The 1st Marine Brigade would relieve the 77th in the south and continue to patrol the southern half of Guam. As the attack gained momentum northward and the island widened, the 1st would join in the drive to the island's extreme north coast.

When the 3rd Division reached Ordot, in the center of their zone, the 3/21 Marines smashed into enemy troops and one of their pillboxes. Marines destroyed fifteen Japanese troops and two light tanks with M1s and bazookas.

The 3/3 Marines had the honor of liberating Agana. Riflemen entered the town ruins and tread carefully, sizing up dusty, stark building walls for snipers. A few enemy snipers emerged from behind concrete outcroppings before falling back into eternity. The Japanese in Agana were stragglers, wounded or foolish enough to stay. In one of the houses, a Marine opened the closet to reveal a Japanese officer with sword in hand. The Marine slammed the door, fired at it with his automatic rifle, and didn't even bother to look again. The majestic and beautiful Plaza de Espana was back in American hands less than twenty minutes after Marines entered the town. By noon, it was secured.

Japanese light tank in a crater

The 3rd Marines advanced along the Agana-Pago Road. At 1340 they caught up with the 21st Marines after several engagements with snipers, pillboxes, and tanks. By 1500, the 9th Marines on the division's right were across the road and had seized the remaining portion of the highway. It was a hard-surfaced road with two lanes crossing the island's midriff. The Agana-Pago Road was vital to liberating Guam.

After the historic rescue of the island's capital at Agana, the 3/3 Marines advanced with relative ease. Before nightfall, the battalion had seized over 1,500 yards of roads and trails needed to defend the strategic strong points of Barrigada and Finegayan.

General Turnage got close to the Tiyan Airfield and the village of San Antonio on August 1, but his advance was seriously slowed by mines. It took the steady hands and cool skill of the bomb disposal specialists of the 25th Naval Construction Battalion and the 19th Marine Engineers to reduce and remove those obstacles.

Many historians and those who were there consider taking the cross-island Agana-Paco Road a major factor in guaranteeing the northern advance's success. Its capture solved several logistical problems for the 77th. The Army division had no roads heading north and desperately needed a road to resupply their troops as they came down from the hills and cut their way through the jungle. Army front-line troops were running low on supplies—especially water. General Bruce promised his soldiers a hot breakfast as soon as the Marines would give him the road. Not long after, trucks were thick on the road, even while the Seabees and engineers enlarged and repaired it.

The 77th moved out at daylight on July 31. Enemy resistance to the Army advance was insignificant. In under two hours, the Army division had secured the cross-island road in their zones. They also rescued over 3,000 Guamanians at the Japanese detention camp in Asinan. Now unopposed, the 77th were across the Pago River. Residents of the area said the Japanese fled to Barrigada, where intelligence had expected the enemy to hide. The mountain was covered by a jungle, 650 feet high, and it dominated the area.

General Bruce ordered the 77th to capture Barrigada. They would keep contact with the 3rd Marine Division on the left and push through the village and then the one mile to seize Mount Barrigada. The village was a clearing fully swept with defensive machine-gun fire. In the same clearing was a much desired well. Capturing it meant everything to the thirsty troops.

On August 2 at 0630, General Bruce dispatched a dozen tanks of the 706th Tank Battalion to reconnoiter the area. As the tanks turned toward the village, the Japanese opened up with a surge of fire.

The stubborn enemy defenders resisted and were determined to stop the assault companies from outflanking them. Heavy artillery support and repeated tank attacks netted only a few yards at a time, but the soldiers kept advancing. By August 4, the 77th Division finally held the village, or what was left of it, along with the precious well.

Captured documents and interviews with prisoners left little doubt that the 77th Division's major obstacle would be the heavily creviced, rugged jungle of Mount Santa Rosa. Seven miles northeast of Barrigada and close to the ocean on the east coast.

But first, well-armed enemy outposts blocking the way had to be destroyed. Yigo and Finegayan would be assaulted first. While each outpost promised a bloody battle and several casualties, General Geiger used the 77th to annihilate Yigo and then take Santa Rosa. The 3rd Marine Division would capture Finegayan and take the rest of northern Guam. He brought up General Shepherd's brigade to assist in the final drive. The 1/22 Marines would protect the force beachhead line and care for the Guamanians while still hunting down enemy stragglers in the south.

The 1/22 Marines aggressively sought out enemy holdouts. They also brought terrified Guamanians into friendly compounds and provide security for those who decided to remain in their homes and work their ranches. By August 2, Marine patrols approached Talofofo Bay on the southern coast. They found another 2,000 natives, still terrified of the Japanese, and directed them to a compound that promised safety and a small amount of comfort. In their own residential and farm areas, many Guamanians could still call upon this civil affairs section for protection, medicine, food, and shelter. This civil care was vital to the American occupation now that the island was once again under the American flag.

During the night of August 2, the 12th Marines delivered 750 rounds of harassing and interdictory fire onto the roads and trails that the division would encounter around Finegayan. At dawn, Marines moved in and passed Tinian Airfield. At 0700, they encountered a block at the crossroads approaching the Finegayan village. This terrain favored the Japanese with the excellent fields of fire. After the enemy position was finally overrun with tanks, Lieutenant Colonel Carey Randall said that these defenses were: "the toughest he had faced on Guam."

The battle for Finegayan was the last major battle for the 3rd Division on Guam. The Japanese made it a fight to remember. A 3rd Division armored reconnaissance patrol headed for Ritidian Point, on the northern tip of the island, ran into Japanese defenses. The enemy had dug in on the Finegayan trails and bristled with antitank weapons and artillery pointed at the patrol. Americans were bruised and surprised and did the Japanese some harm—but canceled their mission and withdrew.

The enemy was feisty at Finegayan. In a brave thrust, they dispatched two medium tanks skirting the crossroads of the 9th Marines at Junction 177. Nearly invulnerable to Marine fire, they shot up the area and got away. Another tank force rumbled down over a mortar barrage that seemed like the beginning of a counterattack. Marine artillery stalled the enemy effort, and Japanese tanks were driven off but survived to reappear another day.

LIBERATION OF GUAM

On August 4, new front lines and maneuvers were established to keep the pressure on General Obata and his remaining holdouts. During the afternoon, the brigade reached its northern assembly area, and General Shepherd set up his command post near the small town of San Antonio. In this final advance north, the brigade would be on the left with its inland flank less than a mile from the western beaches. The 3rd Division would advance in the center and deploy its units into a three-regiment front that would swerve to the east, taking in the whole northern end of the island and supporting the 77th Infantry Division.

The enemy defenders faced overwhelming odds. General Bruce's soldiers attacked Mount Santa Rosa and destroyed any remaining Japanese. The Army had priority of fire from air support, corps artillery, and naval gunfire.

The Marines also made strides to end the campaign. The 21st Marines progressed, while the 9th Marines kept running into a denser jungle. It was a tangled mess where tanks passed each other within fifteen feet without knowing where the other was. The division sped up its advance in battalion columns. By August 6, they'd advanced over 5,000 yards along the road to Ritidian Point. The end of the island and the end of the battle for Guam. That night, the 3rd Division made visual contact with the 77th—wherever the jungle would allow.

The Army Air Force bombing, Marine artillery, and naval shelling had been going on in enemy areas for days. Night fighters also supported the advance. Even in darkness, the enemy defenders had no protection or reprieve. By August 6, General Obata's defensive line across Guam was shattered and overrun. Only isolated pockets of enemy troops were left on the island.

American commanders still could not say when the fight for Guam would be over. The assault on Mount Santa Rosa began at noon on August 7. In the rumble of artillery and rattle of tanks, the 77th took Yigo, the gateway to Santa Rosa, and continued its wheeling maneuver. Tanks and infantry overran machine gun positions while bulldozers blazed trails. By the night of August 7, the 77th was dug into positions and ready for the final attack on the mountain. The Japanese counterattacks still did not come. The rapid American advance accompanied by heavy artillery likely stalled any enemy counterattack.

On August 8, the northern half of Mount Santa Rosa was in American hands, and troops moved to secure the rest of the mountain. By early afternoon, the Army reached the cliffs of the sea and looked right down into the ocean. The infantry had also completed an enveloping move by taking the northern slopes of Mount Santa Rosa.

Over 650 enemy bodies were found after the two-day battle. Estimates of enemy troops at Santa Rosa had been as high as 5,000. This meant enemy troops in significant numbers still infested the jungle terrain everywhere on Guam. Worse, several enemy tanks were unaccounted for. Japanese survivors from the battle drifted into the 9th Marines' lines on the Army flank and slowed the regiment's advance. Sharp-eyed Marines noted significant enemy movement at a hill in the Army's zone —General Obata's command post.

The 3rd Marines on the left advanced through light enemy opposition. A twenty-man roadblock held up the Marines but was quickly destroyed. After searching through a corridor, Marines found the bodies of thirty dead Guamanians. They were beheaded.

The brigade had it easier on the far west flank. They encountered light resistance and advanced along a fairly good trail. On August 8, the 22nd Marines finally reached Ritidian Point at the islands' northernmost tip. Moving along a twisted cliff trail to the beach, Marines encountered less than aggressive Japanese defenses, which they quickly overran. The 1st Marine Brigade had the honor of being first to reach both the southernmost point of the island and Guam's northernmost tip at Ritidian Point.

Marines patrolled the area they occupied but found few Japanese. General Geiger ordered the naval gunfire to be reduced, while the Saipan-based P-47s made their last bombing and strafing runs at Ritidian Point. The 22nd Marines scoured the cliffs below and along the beaches searching for enemy caves. On August 9, at 1800, General Shepherd declared all organized resistance had ceased in his zone.

But it wasn't that easy for the 3rd Marines. On August 9, near Tarague, the regiment was hit by an enemy tank and mortar attack. Marine antitank grenades and bazooka rockets were wet and ineffective against the enemy assault. The Japanese soldiers blazed away with impunity before ducking back into the woods. When Major Bill Culpepper, commanding the 2nd Battalion, counted heads, he noted his Marines hadn't suffered one-single-casualty.

The 9th Marines had advanced to Pati Point on the northeastern tip of the island. Intelligence reported that 2,000 Japanese troops were held up at Savana Grand in a wild tract of jungle and coconut trees and high grass near the coast. Command did not want to risk any casualties so close to the campaign's end and called in artillery—2,275 rounds. Japanese survivors were routed, and either killed or taken prisoner.

The final American positions were formed along the coast, and by nightfall on August 8, the 9th Marines waved to the soldiers of the 77th patrolling to their south.

General Geiger wanted the pocket of enemy tanks destroyed before he would declare Guam secure. This had to be completed by the 10th, because Admiral Nimitz was scheduled to arrive on a visit. Major Culpepper's 2/3 Marines were tasked with finding and eliminating the remaining enemy tanks. At 0730, Culpepper's battalion and a platoon of American Sherman tanks found two enemy medium tanks firing 400 yards up the trail from the Marines. The Shermans left their counterparts hunks of burning metal when they were finished. Seven more enemy medium tanks were abandoned. The remaining Japanese troops withdrew to the cliffs and were destroyed.

On August 10 at 1130, after hearing the remaining Japanese tanks were destroyed, General Geiger declared all organized resistance on Guam over. A great day for the Guamanians—their island was theirs again.

This was also the end for General Obata. On the morning of August 11, when the general knew his headquarters had been discovered, and the enemy was coming for him, he signaled a message to the Emperor: "We continue this desperate battle. We now have only our bare hands to fight with. The holding of Guam is now hopeless. Our souls will defend the island to the very end. I am overwhelmed with sorrow for the families of the many slain officers and men. I pray for the prosperity of the Empire."

The 77th made its assault on Obata's headquarters, supported by demolition squads and tanks. Enemy defenders killed seven Americans and wounded fifteen others before they were destroyed and buried in the rubble of blown caves and emplacements. It is still unclear if General Obata committed suicide or was killed in those last hours of the battle for Guam.

General Henry Larsen assumed command of Guam on August 15. Under him were the forces of the 3rd Marine Division to continue the mopping up.

A terrible cost for the Japanese on Guam was the already

counted 10,970 bodies. And there were still supposedly 10,000 more Japanese on the island. At first, some of the enemy defenders fought in staged ambushes, and some sniped at Americans, but soon the remaining Japanese sought only one thing—food. Most others fled when encountered. The Japanese had no central command. They died of dysentery, starved, became too weak to run, and finally blew themselves up with the one precious grenade they saved to take their own lives. American patrols were aggressive in killing and capturing near eighty Japanese sailors and soldiers a day. A few daring Japanese snuck into Marine food storage areas at night.

In addition to the battlefield casualties, over 8,800 Japanese were captured or killed on Guam between August 1944 and the end of the war on August 1945.

The twenty-one-day Guam campaign ended on August 10. Marine units of the III Amphibious Corps reported 5,308 wounded and 1,567 men killed in action. The 77th Division's casualties were 843, with 177 soldiers killed.

The Marines and Army ran a closely-knit team in the liberation of Guam. General Holland Smith referred to General Bruce's troops as "the 77th Marines."

According to Major Aplington, a battalion commander in the 3rd Marines: "The fatigues are so different from our herringbone utilities and their olive drab ponchos so different from us. But there is no doubt the 77th were good men to have alongside us in a fight, and as a result, we refer to them as the 77th Marine Division."

On August 10, on the same busy day, only hours after Major Culpepper's battalion knocked out the last of the Japanese tanks. The *Indianapolis* steamed into Apra Harbor with Marine Commandant Alexander Vandergrift on board accompanying Admiral Nimitz. On August 15, Nimitz directed his forward headquarters be established on Guam, and from there he directed the rest of the Pacific War.

Soon after, from airfields on Guam and Tinian, B-29s blasted the Japanese home islands. While there was still more hard fighting to come, Peleliu, Iwo Jima, and Okinawa, the end of the war was less than one year away.

MARINE PRESENCE ON GUAM

The signing of the Treaty of Paris in 1899, after the Spanish-American war, made Guam and the Philippines territorial possession of the United States.

On June 21, 1898, First Lieutenant John "Handsome Jack" Myers led a party of Marines ashore from the cruiser *Charleston* to accept the surrender of the Spanish forces. The Spanish authorities at the time didn't even know a state of war existed between Spain and the US.

This began a long Marine presence on Guam. Ferdinand Magellan discovered this southernmost island in the Mariana's chain in 1521, but it was not occupied until 1688 when Spanish soldiers and priests established a small mission.

When control of the other Mariana Islands, including Tinian and Saipan, were given to Japan in 1919, Guam became an isolated and highly valuable American outpost in a sea of Japanese.

Guam is thirty-five miles long, nine miles wide at its widest, and four at its narrowest. It's shaped like a peanut and has a year-long temperature of 79 degrees Fahrenheit. In the early morning of December 10, 1941, Guam was captured by a fierce Japanese attack from her sister island of Saipan.

Once Captain George McMillan, Governor of Guam, realized he would not receive reinforcements or relief, he surrendered to the Japanese naval forces. One of his biggest concerns was the fate of the 25,000 Guamanians who would suffer if a strong defense was mounted. McMillan believed the situation was hopeless. He ordered the 223 Marines at Sumay on Orote Peninsula to lie down their arms. Even after giving orders to surrender, Marines suffered sixty-one casualties in two days of fighting and bombing.

GUAM WAR DOGS

Toward the end of summer 1942, the Marine Corps experimented with the use of dogs in war. While new to the Corps, dogs in war were not a new idea in warfare. Since ancient times, dogs have served fighting men. Romans used heavy mastiffs with armored collars to attack their enemies' legs, forcing them to lower their shields.

On Guam, Lieutenant Bill Putney commanded the 1st Dog Platoon and was the veterinarian for all war dogs on Guam. Along with Lieutenant Bill Taylor in charge of the 2nd Dog Platoon, they had sixty war dogs, ninety handlers, two war dog corpsmen, three kennelmen, and ten NCOs. In total, about three hundred and fifty war dogs served in the Guam operation.

Handlers were trained scouts and skilled dog specialists. Dog and man searched out the enemy, awaited his arrival, and caught him by surprise around the Marine perimeter while on patrol. Dogs were used to find snipers, rout stragglers, and search out pillboxes and caves. They also ran messages and protected Marine's foxholes just like they would at private homes. The dogs walked, slept, ate, and lived with their handlers. The presence of dogs on the line promised Marines a decent night's sleep. War dogs were quick to alert their handlers when enemy troops came close.

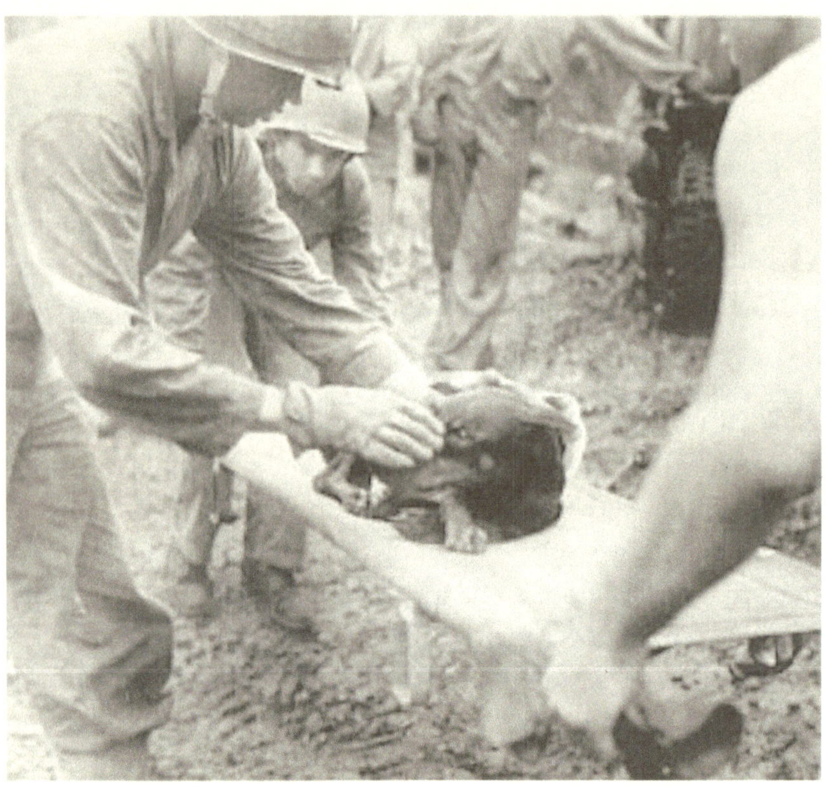

Early in the Guam operation, several dogs were injured or killed by machine-gun fire and incoming mortars. This loss devastated the Marines. When dogs were wounded, Marines made a point of getting them to the rear as fast as possible. In the recapture of Guam, war dogs suffered forty-five casualties, with twenty-five dogs killed.

Guam served as a staging area for war dogs. Eighty-five percent of the Marine Corps' war dogs were Doberman Pinschers, and the rest were German Shepherds.

At the end of the Pacific War, the Marine Corps had over 500 war dogs. Four hundred and ninety dogs were deprogrammed, a process that could take a year. Then they were returned to their owners or given to their handlers. Only four dogs could not be returned to their masters because they remained "incorrigible" and considered too unsafe for living a civilian life, even after extensive retraining.

3RD MARINE DIVISION INSIGNIA

The 3rd Marine Division insignia was adopted on August 25, 1943, while the division trained on Guadalcanal for the upcoming invasion of Bougainville. The insignia comprised a caltrop on a triangular, gold-bordered, scarlet shield. Historically, the caltrop was a medieval defensive weapon used against both infantry and cavalry. 

In Middle-Age warfare, large numbers of caltrops were scattered by defenders on the ground in front of an approaching enemy. The four-prong forged iron caltrop was designed so that no matter which way it landed when thrown on the ground—one point would be up with the other three points supporting it.

When used on the insignia, the caltrop represented the 3rd Marine Division and the motto painted on the drums carried by the Continental Marines in the American Revolution: Don't Tread on Me.

COLT M1911A1 PISTOL

Standard issue to many Marine officers, noncommissioned officers, and specialists not armed with an M1 carbine or a rifle during World War II. Since 1911, this pistol had served its Marine owners and other service members armed with it well.

The first M1911 pistols were issued to the Marine Corps in 1912. Shortly afterward, the Marine Corps fielded this pistol exclusively. Colt had manufactured over 55,000 pistols by the time the US entered World War I, but there was still not enough, and some units of the American Expeditionary Force were armed with revolvers. This caused more than half a million M1911s to be produced before 1926, when the M1911 was modified and improved into the new pistol—M1911A1.

The new modifications gave the pistol a contoured handgrip, longer grip safety, and a shorter and serrated trigger with wider sites. Around 1.8 million of the newer M1911A1s were produced and others upgraded to meet the new specs during World War II.

The Pacific War also meant further changes for the pistol. Among these was altering the finish from the common shiny blue-black to a dull gray known as "Parkerization," designed to give the pistol a more non-reflective and matte surface. The wartime M1911A1 also had checkered plastic grips instead of a molded rubber.

Colt couldn't keep up with the demand. And so, the following firms were licensed to produce the M1911A1— Singer Sewing Machine Company, Remington Arms Company, and the Union Switch and Signal Company, among others. Remington out produced Colt during wartime years by over half a million pistols.

JOE BLOW STORIES

Marine Combat Correspondent Cyril O'Brien wrote this account of Chonito Ridge after being in the field and witnessing the battle. It was published in the United States not long after the event "and always after families were notified of the death or wounding of any Marines mentioned."

July 24 on Guam: The first frontal attack on the steep Chonito Ridge was made one hour after the Marine landing.

Lieutenant Jim Gallo led an infantry squad and was within ten yards of the ridge's tip when the crest exploded with machine-gun fire. In the face of it, the Marine company tried its first assault. The company was thrown back before they made forty yards.

For fifty hours, the company remained on the naked slope.

They tried to storm the Jap entrenchments less than 100 yards away. After almost being battered to destruction, the resilient Marines saw another company take the ridge from the rear.

Failing the first rush, they formed a flimsy defense line less than fifty yards from the enemy. Cover was scarce. Marines had only tufts of grass to shield them. Japs rolled grenades down the crest and blasted Marines with knee mortars from over the summit.

The company commander led a second attack under cover of dusk. As Marines rose, machine-gun fire swept into them. The commander and three Marines reached the crest. The last fifty feet were nearly vertical. Marines grasped roots and dug their feet into the soft earth to keep from falling down the incline.

The commander went over the ridge—but never came back. The remaining three Marines were ripped apart by crossfire. One saved himself by jumping into an enemy foxhole.

Beaten again, the company withdrew to a small ravine and stayed all night. One of the wounded Marines, shot through both legs, begged for morphine. Another Marine's thigh was ripped open by shell fragments. One PFC, with a dry, swollen tongue, tried to whisper the range of an enemy sniper.

On the morning of the 22nd, with just a third of their original number remaining, the company rushed the hillside again.

Lieutenant Gallo led the assault on the left flank of the hill but was thrown back. Sergeant Charles Bomar, 33 years old from Houston Texas, and nine Marines tried to take the slope's right ground. Five were killed instantly as they left the ravine. Bomar and three Marines finally reached the top of the slope.

Japs again rolled grenades down the incline. One exploded under the chest of a nearby Marine, taking his head clean off.

Another grenade bounced off the helmet of the sergeant—lucky for him it was a dud.

Marines charged into the Jap entrenchment. Sergeant Bomar killed an enemy machine gunner with the butt of his carbine. The assistant gunner exploded a grenade against his body. The blast knocked the Marines out of the hole, and they fell back into vacated enemy foxholes. A lieutenant who had just come to join them was shot right between the eyes by a sniper. Bomar turned and killed the sniper with his M1 carbine.

Unable to hold their positions, Sergeant Bomar and his Marines returned to the shelter of the ravine. They were all that remained of their shattered company. They waited for nearly twenty-four hours until darting Marines on top of the ridge showed Chonito had been taken from the rear.

Stories like these were known as "Joe blow" stories. Written to improve the morale of the men. Many stories like this were printed in hometown newspapers and then clipped and sent to troops in the Pacific, who could then see their efforts were appreciated at home.

GENERAL ROY GEIGER

Roy Geiger and several other general officers in the Guam invasion force were World War I veterans. Geiger was an early Marine Corps aviator. He was the fifth Marine to become a naval aviator in 1917 and forty-ninth in the naval service to get his wings.

He went to France in July of that year and commanded a squadron of the 1st Marine Aviation Force. After the Great War, he continued his education at the Army Command School in Fort Leavenworth in 1924 and then to the Naval War College in Newport, Rhode Island, from 1939 to 1941.

In August 1941, he became the commanding general of the 1st Marine Aircraft Wing and led it at Guadalcanal during the hard days from September to November 1942.

After returning to Washington in 1943, he was made

Director of Aviation until General Charles Barnett's death when Geiger was rushed out to the Pacific to assume command and direct the landings at Augusta Bay, off of Bougainville, on November 1, 1943.

He was the first Marine aviator to lead a large ground command, re-designated as III Amphibious Corps in April 1944.

General Geiger led this organization in the liberation of Guam in July 1944, then onto Peleliu and then as part of the 10th Army in Okinawa's invasion.

In July 1945, at the end of the Okinawan operation, General Geiger assumed command of the Fleet Marine Force at Pearl Harbor. In November 1946, he returned to Marine headquarters in Washington and died in January the next year.

GENERAL ALLEN TURNAGE

Commissioned in 1913, Turnage was sent off to France as commanding officer of the 5th Machine Gun Battalion in the 5th Marine Brigade. After serving honorably in the Great War and returning to the US, Turnage was given an assortment of duties from sea duty and overseas assignments.

In 1935, he reported as the director of The Basic School in the Philadelphia Navy Yard. When World War II began, he commanded Camp Lejeune in North Carolina, and its training center. He was responsible for the organization and training of two regimental combat teams slated for duty with the 3rd Marine Division.

In September 1943, he became commander of the 3rd Marine Division. General Turnage led the division in the landing at Bougainville and the recapture of Guam.

At the end of the war, he became assistant commander of the Marine Corps. General Turnage's last assignment was the command of Fleet Marine Force at Pearl Harbor.

He retired in 1948 as a four-star general at just under 57 year old. He died peacefully in October 1971.

GENERAL ANDREW BRUCE

Andrew Bruce was a native of Missouri and a graduate of Texas A&M in 1916. In June 1917, he was commissioned as an Army second lieutenant. His involvement with the Marine Corps goes back to the Great War when he fought in France at Verdun and in the Aisne-Marne offensive at Soissons. He hiked into Germany with the rest of the 2nd Division and became part of the occupation force.

After returning from WWI, he had a mix of command, staff, and school assignments. At the beginning of World War II then Colonel Bruce headed the Army's tank destroyer school at Camp Meade in Maryland.

Bruce assumed command of the 77th Infantry Division in May 1943. The division first saw combat along with the 3rd Marines and the 1st Provisional Marine Brigade on Guam.

Afterward, they landed at Leyte Gulf in the Philippines to assist in that operation.

General Bruce's 77th Infantry Division again fought with Marines landing on April 1, 1945, at Okinawa. Bruce's 77th and the Marine 1st Division joined in once again to assault the enemy's front lines. General Bruce retired as a three-star general and died peacefully in 1969.

GENERAL LEMUEL SHEPHERD

In his final year at the Virginia Military Institute, Lemuel Shepherd had not yet graduated when he was commissioned into the Marine Corps for the Great War. He sailed off to France as a junior officer in the Marine's 4th Brigade. He saw considerable action in the war. He was wounded twice at Belleau Wood. After recovering from his injuries, he rejoined his regiment in time for the St. Mihiel and Meuse-Argonne offensives.

Shepherd served in the Army of Occupation in Germany. After returning home, he became aide to the commandant and served at the White House.

During the period between wars, he had a mix of staff, school, and command assignments. He assumed command of the 9th Marines in March 1942, taking them overseas as part of the 3rd Marine Division. Upon his promotion to flag rank in July 1943, he was assigned to the 1st Marine Division as assistant division commander.

He participated in Operation Backhander, the Cape Gloucester operation. He then assumed command of the 1st Provisional Marine Brigade in May 1944 and led them in Guam's landings and liberation.

After Guam, General Shepherd received a second star, took command of the 6th Marine Division, and took part in the Okinawan landings.

Shepherd commanded the Fleet Marine Force in the first two years of the Korean War and then was chosen to serve as the 20th Commandant of the Marine Corps.

General Lemuel Shepherd lived to the ripe old age of 94 and died peacefully in 1990.

GENERAL ROBERT CUSHMAN

Robert Cushman was a 29-year-old colonel, commanding the 2/9 Marines on Guam. He was awarded the Navy Cross for his extraordinary heroism during the months of July and August in 1944.

Part of his citation reads: "His battalion was ordered to seize and hold a vigorously defended and organized enemy point that had been holding up the advance for days. Colonel Cushman repulsed many Japanese counterattacks and directed the attacks of his battalion. He exposed himself fearlessly to enemy rifle, mortar, and machine-gun fire in order to remain on the front lines and get first-hand knowledge of the enemy situation.

"After three days of bitter fighting, culminating into a heavy enemy counterattack that pushed back the flank of his battalion, he led a platoon into the gap, and placing it in for defense—repelled the enemy forces. His inspiring leadership, devotion to duty, and courage contributed to the destruction of one Japanese Battalion and the rout of another."

On January 1, 1972, General Cushman became the 25th Commandant of the Marine Corps. Four years later, Cushman retired and General Louis Wilson, who commanded a company of Cushman's 2/9 Marines on Guam, became the 26th Commandant of the Marine Corps.

HEROES ON GUAM

When Captain Louis Wilson served as the commanding officer of a rifle company attached to the 2/9 Marines at Fonte Hill on Guam on July 26, 1944, he was tasked to take that portion of the hill within his zone of action. Captain Wilson started his attack in midafternoon and pushed up the rugged, open terrain against horrific machine gun and rifle fire

for nearly 400 yards before successfully capturing his objective.

He took command of other disorganized units and motorized equipment in addition to his own company. He also organized night defenses in the face of continuous hostile fire. Although wounded three times in five hours, he completed his disposition of men and guns before retiring to the company command post for medical attention.

Soon after, the Japanese launched a series of savage counterattacks that lasted all night. He rejoined his unit and repeatedly exposed himself to a merciless hail of shrapnel and bullets. He dashed fifty yards into the open to rescue a wounded Marine lying helpless on the front lines.

He fought fiercely in hand-to-hand encounters. He led his men in a brutally waged battle for over ten hours, resiliently holding his line and repelling the fanatical enemy counter thrusts until he destroyed the last efforts of the hard-pressed enemy early the next morning.

He reorganized a seventeen-man patrol and advanced upon a strategic slope that was essential to the security of his position. He boldly defied intense mortar and machine-gun fire, which killed thirteen of his men, and advanced relentlessly with his patrol's remnants to seize the vital ground. By his truly heroic leadership, daring combat tactics, and bravery in the face of impossible odds, Captain Wilson succeeded in capturing and holding strategic high ground in his sector. He was essential to the success of the regimental mission and in the destruction of over 300 Japanese troops. He was awarded the Medal of Honor for his conspicuous gallantry and risking his life above and beyond the call of duty.

Private First Class Frank Witek served with the 1/9 Marines during the Battle of Finegayan on Guam on August 3, 1944. After his rifle platoon was stalled by surprise heavy Japanese fire from hidden positions, Private First Class Witek bravely remained standing to fire a full magazine from his Browning automatic rifle at point-blank range into a depression housing Japanese troops. He killed eight enemy troops and enabled the greater part of his platoon to take cover.

During his platoon's withdrawal, he again remained and

safeguarded a wounded comrade, courageously returning enemy fire until the stretcher bearers could arrive.

He then covered the evacuation by sustained fire, moving backward toward his lines. When his platoon was again pinned down by hostile machine-gun fire, Witek, on his initiative, moved forward boldly to the reinforcing tanks and infantry, throwing hand grenades, and firing as he advanced within five yards of enemy positions.

He destroyed a hostile machine-gun emplacement and an additional seven enemy troops before an enemy rifleman struck him down. His courageous and inspiring actions helped to reduce enemy firepower and enabled his platoon to keep their objective. Private First Class Witek was a credit to the United States naval service. He gallantly gave his life for his country and was posthumously awarded the Medal of Honor.

Private First Class Luther Skaggs was a squad leader with the mortar section of a rifle company in the 3/3 Marines on the Asan-Adelup beachhead on Guam on July 22, 1944. When a section leader was killed under a heavy mortar barrage shortly after the landing, Private First Class Skaggs took command and led

the section through intense fire for over 200 yards to a position where they could deliver effective coverage.

He bravely defended the critical position against strong enemy counterattacks. Private First Class Skaggs was critically wounded when a Japanese grenade was lobbed into his foxhole and exploded, shattering the lower part of his left leg. He quickly acted and applied an improvised tourniquet. He propped up in his foxhole and returned enemy fire with his rifle and hand grenades for eight hours.

After the enemy had been destroyed, he crawled, unassisted, to the rear. Calm and uncomplaining throughout this period, Private First Class Skaggs was a heroic example of courage and resilience to other wounded men. For his courageous leadership and inspiring devotion to duty, he was awarded the Medal of Honor.

Private First Class Leonard Mason served with the 2/3 Marines also on the Asan-Adelup Beachhead on Guam on July 22, 1944. He suddenly took fire from two enemy machine guns less than fifteen yards away while clearing out hostile positions, holding up the advance of his platoon through a narrow gully. Mason, alone and completely on his own initiative, climbed out of the gully and moved parallel toward the rear of the enemy position. Although fired upon immediately by hostile riflemen from a higher position and wounded in the arm and shoulder, Private First Class Mason pressed forward. He reached his objective when he was hit again by a burst of enemy machine-gun fire. This caused a critical wound to which he later succumbed. With a valiant disregard for his own life, he persevered and cleared out the hostile position. He killed five Japanese and wounded another before rejoining his platoon.

This heroic act in the face of certain death enabled his platoon to accomplish its mission and reflects the highest credit upon Private First Class Mason. He gallantly gave his life for his country. He was posthumously awarded the Medal of Honor.

* * *

Building a relationship with my readers is one of the best things about writing. I occasionally send out emails with details on new releases and special offers. If you'd like to join my free readers group and never miss a new release, just go to daniel-wrinn.com and you can sign up for the list.

REFERENCES

Information available for researching the World War II Pacific Theater is vast. I've listed my main reference sources below. Websites, newspaper articles, and even History Channel documentaries also contributed to my research.

Chapin, Captain John C. "Breaching the Marianas - United States Marine Corps." U.S. Marine Corps Reserve (RET), 1994.

Chen, C. Peter. "Mariana Islands Campaign and the Great Turkey Shoot." World War II Database. Lava Development, LLC, 2004.

Chen, C. Peter. "Palau Islands and Ulithi Islands Campaign," World War II Database. Lava Development, LLC, 2007.

Denfeld, D. Colt, and Eugene L. Rasor. "Hold the Marianas: The Japanese Defense of the Islands." *The Journal of Military History*, 1997.

Drea, Edward J. "An Allied Interpretation of the Pacific War." 1998.

Drea, Edward J. Essay. In *In the Service of the Emperor: Essays on the Imperial Japanese Army*. Lincoln, Neb.: University of Nebraska Press, 2003.

Dull, Paul s. *A Battle History of the Imperial Japanese Navy, 1941-1945*. Annapolis: Naval Institute Press, 1978.

Dyer, George Carroll. *The Amphibians Came to Conquer: the Story of Admiral Richmond Kelly Turner*. Washington, D.C, Dept. of the Navy,: United States Government Printing Office – via Hyperwar Foundation, 1973.

Gailey, Harry A. *The Liberation of Guam, 21 July-10 August 1944*. Novato, CA: Presidio, 1988.

Gailey, Harry A. *Peleliu, 1944*. Annapolis, MD: Nautical & Aviation Pub. Co. of America, 1983. ISBN 0-933852-41-X.

Gnam, Carl. "Marine Fight for Tinian: A squabble between a general and an admiral led to 'the most perfect amphibious operation of the Pacific War.'" Warfare History Network, June 16, 2020.

Goldberg, Harold J. *D-Day in the Pacific The Battle of Saipan*. Bloomington: Indiana University Press, 2007.

Guillaume, Marine. "Napalm in US Bombing Doctrine and Practice, 1942-1975." Sciences Po portal, December 10, 2016.

Hallas, James H. *The Devil's Anvil: the Assault on Peleliu*. Westport, CT: Praeger, 1994.

Harwood, Richard. "A Close Encounter: The Marine Landing on Tinian." 1994.

Hoffman, Major Carl W., USMC. *Saipan: the Beginning of the End*. Washington, D.C.: Historical Division, U.S. Marine Corps, 1950.

Hoffman, Major Carl W., USMC. *The Seizure of Tinian:* Washington, DC: Historical Division, Headquarters, U.S. Marine Corps, 1951.

O'Brien, Cyril J. "Liberation: Marines in the Recapture of Guam", Marine Corps Historical Center, United States Marine Corps, 1994.

O'Brien, Francis. *Battling for Saipan*. New York: Ballantine Books, 2003.

Rottman, Gordon L. *Saipan & Tinian 1944: Piercing the Japanese Empire*. Oxford: Osprey, 2004.

shed light on real people and events from one of the greatest conflicts in human history.

• **WWI: Tales from the Trenches**, a sweeping and eerily realistic narrative which explores the struggles and endless dangers faced by soldiers in the trenches during the heart of WWI

• **Broken Wings**, a powerful and heroic story about one pilot after he was shot down and spent 72 harrowing days on the run deep behind enemy lines

• **Mission to Ireland**, which explores the devious and cunning plan to smuggle a ship loaded with weapons to incite an Irish rebellion against the British

• And **Journey into Eden**, a fascinating glimpse into the lesser-known battles on the harsh and unforgiving Mesopotamian Front

World War I reduced Europe's mightiest empires to rubble, killed twenty million people, and cracked the foundations of our modern world. In its wake, empires toppled, monarchies fell, and whole populations lost their national identities.

Each of these stories brings together unbelievable real-life WWI history, making them perfect for casual readers and history buffs alike. If you want to peer into the past and unearth the incredible stories of the brave soldiers who risked everything, then this book is for you.

WINGS OF VICTORY: WORLD WAR II ADVENTURES IN A WAR-TORN EUROPE

"Historical fiction with a realistic twist." – Reviewer

Thrilling World War II adventures like you've never seen them before.

As the Nazis invade Europe on a campaign for total domination, a brutal war begins to unfold which will change the course of the world forever—and John Archer finds himself caught in the middle of it. When this amateur pilot joins the Allied war effort and is tasked with a series of death-defying missions which place him deep into German-occupied territory, his hair-raising adventures will help decide the fate of Europe.

In **War Heroes**, John is caught up in the devastating Nazi invasion of France while on vacation. Teaming up with ambulance driver Barney, John will need his amateur pilot skills and more than a stroke of luck to pull off the escape of the century.

In **Bombs Over Britain**, the Nazis have a plan which could change the course of the entire war . . . unless Archer can stop them. Air-dropped into Belgium on a top-secret mission, Archer must retrieve vital intelligence and make it out alive. But that's easier said than done when the Gestapo are closing in.

And in **Desert Scout**, Archer finds himself stranded beneath the scorching Libyan sun and in a race against time to turn the tide of the war in North Africa. But with the Luftwaffe and the desert vying to finish him off, can he make it out alive?

Packed with action and filled to the brim with suspense, these thrilling stories combine classic adventures with a riveting and historical World War II setting, making it ideal for history buffs and casual readers. If you're a fan of riveting war fiction novels, WW2 aircraft, and the war for the skies, Archer's next adventure will keep you on the edge of your seat.

MONGOOSE BRAVO: VIETNAM: A TIME OF REFLECTION OVER EVENTS SO LONG AGO

"A frank, real, memoir" – Reviewer

Uncover the gritty, real-life story of a Vietnam combat veteran.

With an engaging and authentic retelling of his experiences as an infantry soldier of the B Co., 1/5th 1st Cavalry Division in the Vietnam War, this gripping account details the life and struggles of war in a strange and foreign country.

What started as a way of bringing closure to a grieving mother morphed into a memoir, covering the author's deployment, duty, and eventual return to the United States after the end of the war. Imbued with the emotion that he felt during this conflicted time, along with letters and journal entries from decades ago, this memoir is a testament to the sacrifice that these brave men and women made fighting on foreign soil.

Recounting the tragedies of war and the chaos of combat as an infantry soldier, in the words of the author: "We lived, and fought as a unit, covering each other's backs. Most came home to tell their own stories, many didn't."

If you like gripping, authentic accounts of life and combat during the Vietnam War, then you won't want to miss Mongoose Bravo: Vietnam: A Time of Reflection Over Events So Long Ago.

ABOUT THE AUTHOR

Daniel Wrinn writes Military History & War Stories. A US Navy veteran and avid history buff, Daniel lives in the Utah Wasatch Mountains. He writes every day with a view of the snow capped peaks of Park City to keep him company. You can join his readers group and get notified of new releases, special offers, and free books here: 

www.danielwrinn.com